Hugh a. Taylor's life and the Redefinition of the Archival Universe

by

Jarad Buckwold

Table of Contents

Abstract

Introduction……………………………………………………………………………….1

Chapter One: Early Life in Britain, 1920-1945..…………………………………….....10

Chapter Two: From Oxford to Canada: The Making of an Archivist, 1946-1993………..41

Chapter Three: The Cosmic Prophet………………………………………………….72

Conclusion……………………………………………………………………….......98

Bibliography………………………………………………………………………..101

Abstract

Archival theory in the English-speaking world has a long and varied history. While today, archival theory is permeated with postmodern ideas and philosophies, borrowing from fields as diverse as anthropology and computer science, even just a few decades ago, this was far from the case. In the 1960s and 1970s, and to some extent the 1980s, archival theory served more as a professional guide to best practices and "how to" methodology. This transition was pioneered and strongly influenced by the imaginative and thought-provoking essays of Hugh Alexander Taylor, an English-born Canadian archivist who developed a worldview that positioned archives at centre stage. Taylor was able to do so as a result of his fascination with the works of the media theorist, Marshall McLuhan, whose ideas Taylor found directly applicable to archives and archival theory.

This thesis looks at Taylor's life to learn more about who he was as a person and to historicize him to determine how his life experiences contributed to his revolutionary redefinition of archival theory. It draws on Taylor's family and personal archives to find that a lonely childhood in England directly led to the development both of his inner world of imagination and his need to find connections between various topics, peoples, and events. This need to find connections, in addition to leading his life in the direction it took, created a worldview for Taylor on a cosmic scale that placed archives as the force that connects all of Creation. To create this worldview, Taylor undertook three major redefinitions – of knowledge, reality, and archives – and in doing so, positioned archiving as a quasi-religious act and archivists as the spiritual contemporaries and successors of the shamans and community knowledge keepers of oral-based cultures.

Introduction

The world of archival theory has changed dramatically within the last few decades. It has moved from a predominantly mechanical set of standards and best practices to a more postmodern, philosophical discourse that delves into its own assumptions in order to examine them critically. Though this shift in focus cannot be attributed wholly to a single person, it owes much to Hugh Taylor, the British-born Canadian archivist and recipient of the Order of Canada who was among the first and most vocal to take archival theory beyond a purely mechanical philosophy of best practices to one of complex, postmodern discussions of meaning and reality.

Influenced by the Canadian media theorizer and University of Manitoba graduate, Marshall McLuhan, and a plethora of non-archival authors and philosophers, Taylor conceived of archives as being more than a simple organized group of static evidence. Instead, he took many of McLuhan's and the other thinkers' concepts and built philosophical bridges between their work and archives, seeing how relevant they were for archivists. From this starting point, from the 1970s onward, Taylor dove into the world of postmodern philosophy, stretching it to cosmic proportions, largely before it became prominent throughout academia. His writings influenced archival thinking on a wide range of issues, and not just in Canada, but the entire English-speaking world. On top of this, Taylor's professional career had a great impact on Canadian archives and archivists in its own right. In a career as a professional archivist that spanned from 1951 to 1982, Taylor served in the UK as a city archivist for Leeds and Liverpool, and county archivist for Northumberland, and in Canada as provincial archivist in Alberta, New Brunswick, and Nova Scotia and as Director, Historical Branch, of the then Public

Archives of Canada. In addition to being the driving force behind the creation of the Association of Canadian Archivists (ACA), Canada's national archivists' association, he helped to lay the groundwork for curricula to be developed in archival studies programs at the University of British Columbia and the University of Manitoba, among others.

It is the aim of this thesis first to contextualize Taylor himself by writing about his life, both personal and professional. Once contextualized, Taylor's philosophy will be historicized in relation to his life prior to becoming an archivist and his related social, political, and spiritual views. Several key points will be teased out in order to capture, as closely as another human being can via research, who Taylor was and what he believed, what shone through in his writings, and what archivists, other heritage professionals, and researchers of every bend can take from him to improve themselves professionally, academically, and perhaps even personally. A recurring theme is the relationship between Taylor's upbringing, relations, and feelings, and its connection to his life as an archivist. This thesis will make a special effort to view Taylor's life and philosophy as holistically as possible, attempting to describe and relate Taylor's worldview to his professional life as an archivist.

Chapter One

This chapter delves into Taylor's early life, from his birth, through his childhood, his time in the Royal Air Force (RAF) during the Second World War, until his decision to study history at Oxford, where he would first encounter archives and begin his archival career. In this chapter we will see an imaginative, but very lonely boy who often felt distant and cut off from the world around him, due in large part to his parent's economically driven decision to leave for East Africa, where Taylor's father was working as an engineer. This left Taylor in the care of his eccentric but domineering aunt, an actress who provided Taylor with a strong female presence and imparted to him a love of culture and history, but whose strictness and dramatic lifestyle taught Taylor to hide his emotions behind a mask, making him feel further alienated.

Upon their return, Taylor's parents found a boy who had become isolated and aloof, with no faith in his own abilities or worth as he struggled with doubts about his masculinity. The young Taylor, unable to express himself during this trying period, began to retreat into his own imagination, searching for meaning and ways to connect intellectually and emotionally with the world around him, particularly his father. This, in turn, led Taylor to find meaning in the historicity he perceived around him, from architecture that had survived for countless centuries to historical figures who could be admired and connected to by means of stories and histories that had not just to be memorized, but to be felt emotionally so as to create that connection. This need to feel connected, particularly when it came to history, gravitated towards historical reverence for military symbolism and semiotic productions as a surrogate for Taylor's father, who was himself a World War I veteran, and in Taylor's eyes, everything a British man should be, as well as everything Taylor himself was not.

Finally, this chapter looks at Taylor's decision to enlist in the RAF as a means by which to prove his worth as a man and as a productive citizen of the British Empire. It is here that Taylor gained confidence in himself, in his abilities and in his place in the world. It is also while in the RAF, as a wireless operator, that Taylor became exposed to a form of communication that was both non-verbal and non-textual, setting a course toward his future openness to and interest in media literacy. From his time in the RAF,

Taylor emerged a much more self-possessed human being with a goal in mind: to pursue this interest in history by studying it at Oxford.

Chapter Two

This chapter follows Taylor through his years at Oxford, where he became a much more engaged person, one in awe of the academic environment that encouraged thought and imagination. It was also here at Oxford that Taylor discovered his passion for historical archival records, and where he decided he would become an archivist, getting his first job in archives at the Northamptonshire Records Society. He enjoyed this position so much that he decided to pursue an archival diploma at the University of Liverpool and shortly afterward became the City Archivist in Leeds, then Liverpool, and then became the first County Archivist of Northumberland, the county his parents lived in and the last county in England to establish a county archives.

It was also during this period at Oxford and these various archives that Taylor became involved in the Christian ecumenical movement, which sought unity throughout Christendom, and a retreat from the age-old denominational divisions that divided Christianity. This need to bridge divides continued Taylor's need to feel and by extension generate connections, and it was during his work in this movement that he met his future wife, Daphne, with whom he had three daughters.

The Taylor family emigrated to Canada in 1965 when he became the first Provincial Archivist of Alberta. Upon his arrival, he was situated in a unique intellectual position, coming from the British archival tradition that valued the contextualization and understanding of administrative structures and organization, as understood and espoused by Hilary Jenkinson and his peers.[1] From this, he encountered the Canadian tradition that that saw archives as the domain of the historian, records being but raw materials for historical narratives, but also being more accepting of non-textual records, particularly photographs. Taylor was thus stuck between both of these traditions, making him a unique voice within Canada at the time, as he attempted to meld the two by bringing the British tradition to and combining it with the Canadian. Taylor thus borrowed from and was influenced by many, but was in a sense isolated from other archivists in Canada and thus had no significant, specific archival influences, given the nascent state of archival thinking in Canada at the time.

It was, however, in Alberta that Taylor had the first of two revelations that influenced his thinking profoundly. The first involved an internal redefinition of what records were and what role they played in society after seeing the way a Siksika community revered and honoured a medicine bundle that was being donated to the archives. After a few short years, Taylor then moved to New Brunswick to become that province's first Provincial Archivist. There Taylor discovered McLuhan and experienced his second revelation, entirely redefining the way he thought about knowledge and records.

From New Brunswick, in 1971 Taylor moved on to the then Public Archives of Canada in Ottawa where he became Director of the Historical Branch, which he attempted to restructure in concert with what he had learned from McLuhan. The results, however, were of middling success and quite controversial within the archival community. After a number of years, Taylor decided that he preferred regional settings to

---

[1] For a thorough review of Hilary Jenkinson's pivotal contributions to archival theory, see Terry Cook, "What is Past is Prologue: A History of Archival Ideas Since 1898", *Archivaria* 43 (Spring 1997), 17-63.

that of a national archives, and so he left to become the Provincial Archivist of Nova Scotia in 1978, where he worked up until his retirement in the 1982. This chapter then goes on to discuss Taylor's involvement in the creation of the ACA, his presidency of the Society of American Archivists (SAA), and his role in helping to establish graduate professional education for archivists in archival studies. This chapter closes by touching on Taylor's work as an activist in the environmental and peace movements, particularly his involvement in a nuclear disarmament coalition.

Chapter Three

This final chapter begins with a study of Taylor's writings, attempting to place them within the context of the narrative developed in the previous two chapters. The breadth of Taylor's writings makes a study that encompasses the entire canon of his work impossible in a short thesis. And so I focus on a select few of his writings that either were written at transitional moments in Taylor's life, were seminal works of his that influenced the very nature of his philosophy going forward, or otherwise influenced archival theory at a particular moment in time. This section also shows how Taylor's papers were received at the time, including a rather scathing contemporary critique of Taylor's post-McLuhan methodological tilt.

This section is then followed by three interrelated sections that tease from Taylor's writings how they coalesce to form a cohesive, well-developed, quasi-religious epistemological and ontological position, and what this means for archivists. To do this, three important redefinitions Taylor attempted are discussed: namely, the redefinition of knowledge; the redefinition of reality; and the redefinition of archives. The redefinition of knowledge focuses on Taylor's discovery of McLuhan and the way in which that changed his understanding of what a record is, what could be gleaned from the form of a record, and what the sociocultural adoption of various hegemonic media forms throughout history says about a particular society's collective epistemological discourse. His redefinition of reality focuses on how he used his understanding of archival functions and his redefinition of knowledge to reconceive the human condition (as well as that of nature's) as being inherently archival, which makes its protection, in the form of environmentalism and the peace movement a matter of archival preservation. The last redefinition, that of archives, takes the concepts put forward in the first two redefinitions and repositions archivists not as mere professionals, but as quasi-religious shamans who act as community knowledge keepers in the electronic global village that McLuhan predicted.

Sources

For so influential a theorist, there is a relative dearth of secondary material written about Taylor. There are only three published works that deal with his life, and all three are short and focused solely on Taylor's academic work, providing minimal context about his life outside of and prior to his work as an archivist. In 1992, Canadian archival educator Barbara Craig edited a festschrift for Taylor.[2] It contains no writings by Taylor himself, but does have some biographical information about him in its introduction. A second book edited by Canadian archivists Terry Cook and Gordon Dodds contains a selection of Taylor's most influential articles, along with brief pieces following each of them in which Taylor provided additional information and reflected on his articles from

---

[2] Barbara L. Craig, ed., *The Archival Imagination: Essays in Honour of Hugh A. Taylor* (Ottawa: Association of Canadian Archivists, 1992).

the vantage point of hindsight.³ This collection, too, had brief introductory biographical pieces, but once again, they were of limited scope. Finally, upon Taylor's death in 2005, Terry Cook wrote an obituary that appeared in the ACA's journal, *Archivaria*.⁴ This obituary honouring Taylor was brief as obituaries typically are. It therefore contains only a limited amount of information. This thesis then will be the first extended study of Taylor's ideas and life.

Taylor's family archives or fonds at the Nova Scotia Archives was critical to this thesis. In particular, Taylor's correspondence and scrapbooks were invaluable. There are, however, some significant gaps in the fonds. Taylor's childhood remains shrouded, with very few details or related records. Fortunately, Daphne Taylor was kind enough to provide access to a series of audio recordings that Taylor made in an attempt at autobiography. These recordings go into great detail about Taylor's life until his move to Canada in 1965, focusing on the years prior to World War II. For this reason, they proved an invaluable source of information, particularly for chapter one and the beginning of chapter two. For chapter three, as it discusses Taylor's writings and ideas, I have used his works, as well as writings of those who reacted to or used Taylor's ideas. Some of Taylor's articles were read, but not cited. I have, however, included them in the bibliography both for the reader's reference, and because I do not believe that reading a paper and being influenced by it always results in something worthy of direct citation. It should thus be assumed that any of Taylor's works that appear in the bibliography that were not cited, did nonetheless add to my overall understanding of Taylor's outlook, even

---

[3] Terry Cook and Gordon Dodds, eds., *Imagining Archives: Essays and Reflections by Hugh A. Taylor* (Lanham MD, Society of American Archivists and Association of Canadian Archivists in association with Scarecrow Press, 2003).
[4] Terry Cook, "Hugh A. Taylor, 1920-2005", *Archivaria* 60 (Fall 2005): 275-282.

if that contribution did not yield a linguistic expression. There are a few instances in which Daphne Taylor has provided information to me directly. She was not formally interviewed as part of this thesis, but her assistance on some matters was nonetheless a great help, and she has been cited as such where applicable.

Chapter 1: Early Life in Britain, 1920-1945

To understand the mind of Hugh Taylor, as with any human being, one must look at more than his life at the time when his most characteristic ideas were expressed. Rather, Taylor's life must be looked at as a whole and historicized. As no idea is conceived of and held in a temporal vacuum, it is necessary to look at Taylor's life as a young man during his most formative years. While many of his ideas were not conceived until much later in his life, his early life gives clues as to why he conceived of these ideas the way he did. To use the analogy of a computer – which seems fitting, given Taylor's interest and emphasis on all things digital and electronic – it can be seen as a program unfolding, operating as it has been programed to do, but adapting its operation to user input and changing how it functions as a result. His ideas resulted from the unique intersection of experience over time – the user input – and his genetic happenstance – the programming that regulates how he reacts to his subjective experiences.

Despite all that Taylor accomplished, there is very little written about his life. His professional career is outlined briefly in only two publications. A festschrift, edited by Barbara L. Craig[1] was released in 1992, and a collection of Taylor's most influential essays, along with some of his reflections on them, was edited by Terry Cook and Gordon Dodds in 2003.[2] Both of these works contain brief biographical information about Taylor, but as background information rather than as the focus of study. As well, they deal primarily with Taylor's professional life, touching only on a few details of his life outside that. In addition, an obituary for Taylor written by Terry Cook upon Taylor's death in 2005, gives a brief outline of his life, but focuses primarily on his career and the

---

[1] Craig, ed., *The Archival Imagination: Essays in Honour of Hugh A. Taylor*.
[2] Cook and Dodds, eds., *Imagining Archives: Essays and Reflections by Hugh A. Taylor*.

influence of his ideas rather than their genesis.³ This chapter will seek to rectify the dearth of information on Taylor's life until he entered the archival profession. It will do so by examining his life from childhood to the point at which he began attending Oxford, where he first encountered archives and began his love affair with them and thinking about them. Many themes come out in this analysis: most prominent is that of an isolated, timid boy and young man who felt that he was lacking in both masculinity and respectability, and whose isolation forced him to look inward, towards his imagination, making his interactions with the world around him slightly more abstract than average. This was, again, quite isolating, but as we will see, it created the unique frame of reference that Taylor would later put to use in imagining and reimagining archives and their role in human existence.

The primary source used for this chapter is a series of audio recordings that Taylor created in the 1990s, in which he recites an autobiography that he had originally written in 1985, which was titled, in true Taylor fashion, "Journeys in Space, Journeys in Time: A Poor Attempt at Autobiography". Taylor originally wrote this account of his early life while travelling across Canada via train. I received these audio files from Taylor's wife, Daphne, in 2014. The original written version was deposited in the Taylor Family Archive⁴ at the Nova Scotia Archives, along with the rest of Taylor's papers, but, according to the finding aid, the handwritten original was removed by Taylor on March 27, 1989 so that it could be typed. This would have been necessary due to Taylor's often difficult-to-read writing, a problem that he himself acknowledges in a joke made at the

---

3 Cook, "Obituaries: Hugh A. Taylor, 1920-2005".
⁴ Nova Scotia Archives (hereafter NSA), Taylor Family Archives, MG 1, Vols. 2951-2991, 3129-3159.

outset of the memoir.[5] Whether the autobiographical account was ever typed is unknown, as nothing has since been returned to the archives, but given the fact that Taylor made audio recordings, it is likely that he did not finish, or perhaps never even started typing, opting instead for a medium more appropriate, given his emphasis on the "new orality" of the electronic age. It is unfortunate that so few records of Taylor's early life are available, even in the Taylor Family Archive. There are a few letters, primarily between Taylor and his father, as well as some souvenirs and papers written during his time in the Royal Air Force (RAF), but they are few and far between and are light on details that can be used to form a temporal narrative. As a result, the audio files for Taylor's autobiography are the primary source for his early life.

Early Childhood

Hugh Alexander Taylor was born January 22, 1920 in Chelmsford, Essex County, England. He was born into a middle-class family, the only child of Hugh Lamport Taylor and Enid Essex Taylor. Taylor's father was an engineering officer in the First World War, and although he was "no fire eater, but a reserved gentleman", in true English middle-class fashion, he was nonetheless very proud of his military service.[6] It was all the more disheartening for him, then, when the mass cuts to government funding that took place in the early 1920s – known as Geddes' Axe – saw Hugh Lamport and hundreds of other military officers discharged from service.[7] Having been discharged, Hugh Lamport, Enid Essex and their still very young son moved to Farnborough before moving once again in

---

[5] Hugh A. Taylor, "Journeys in Space, Journeys in Time: A Poor Attempt at Autobiography" (hereafter JSJT; digital copies are in the process of being donated to the University of Manitoba Archives & Special Collections), c. 1990s, MPEG 4 Audio, file 1, 1:00. (This last number in each footnote to this source indicates the time point on the recording where the cited information can be located.)
[6] JSJT, file 3, 23:00.
[7] Ibid., file 1, 3:00.

1925 to Herne Bay in Kent, into what they hoped would be both their dream house and where they would live for many years.[8]

Taylor's father had apprenticed as a marine engineer before the war and after being discharged he continued where he left off, going into business as an engineer. He even patented a specialized type of pump, which he hoped one day to develop. Taylor's mother, on the other hand, was a singer who had, according to her son, a beautiful singing voice which he would often hear and enjoy as she practised her scales daily.[9] Due to medical reasons, Taylor's mother could not have any other children, leaving him as an only child. Even as a young only child, Taylor was already very imaginative and cerebral. In his autobiography, Taylor noted this, saying that "as an only child, you learn early on to use your imagination and make your own world which was anything but a cloud cuckoo land. You learn to deal with imaginary fears and to mix up with other kids."[10] He would often have nightmares in which he would wake up screaming and quite frequently believed he was seeing things in the night that were not there such as fingers darting across drawn curtains.[11] His imagination was fuelled by the classic stories his father would read to him. Some favourites included the works of Hans Christian Andersen, Grimms' Fairy Tales, and Rudyard Kipling.

Despite this imaginative trait that comes with being an only child, as a young boy, Taylor was quite sociable.[12] Children, however, are rarely accepting of those different from themselves and Taylor had to deal with more than his share of bullying throughout his childhood. Some of this was due to his poor eyesight: he had a permanent

---

[8] Ibid.
[9] Ibid., 6:00.
[10] Ibid., 10:30.
[11] Ibid., 6:00.
[12] Ibid., 10:15.

squint that was the result of forceps having been used during his birth – something his mother felt guilty about her whole life. Taylor was also teased because his interests differed from most children's. While other children were becoming interested in sport, Taylor was firmly enthralled by stories, history, and his imagination. For example, when Taylor's father would take him to Rugby games, Taylor would instead go off to play in the ruins of a nearby oast house. These ruins "held mysteries and nameless dangers which only children have a way of creating".[13] As such, Taylor's best friend as a child was a springer spaniel named Teaser, who was like a brother to him.[14]

Despite all this, as a young child Taylor was happy. However, this happiness was shattered in 1926, the year of the UK General Strike, during which Taylor's father served as a special constable, keeping order in the streets. During that year, Hugh Lamport's business partner disappeared with all of the firm's money and he was left penniless. The Taylor family had never been rich – Taylor generally wore hand-me-downs from an older cousin and rarely got new clothes[15] – but now their financial situation was dire and Taylor's father desperately needed a job. At the time, the only place hiring engineers was in East Africa. And so while there, Taylor's parents left him in Herne Bay in the care of his maternal grandmother, where he lived as a boarder for the next year or so. This situation was exacerbated by the near fatal injury to Teaser, who lost his footing while jumping and impaled himself on a fence. The dog never fully recovered and was given to a pier master who did his best to look after him; however, it was felt best that Taylor never see the dog again. Therefore, "at one stroke", Taylor lost both his parents and his

---
[13] Ibid.
[14] Ibid., 8:00.
[15] Ibid., 10:15.

best friend.[16] After such an emotionally jarring situation, the need to retreat into imagination would likely only have grown stronger. The openness of his mind and the philosophical slant of his thoughts helped him. Later in life he recalled this situation, saying, "I think I began to learn at this time to be philosophical about setbacks." He decided to make the best of them.[17]

After his parents left for Africa, Taylor began attending a preparatory school where he was subjected to a severe bullying, both from the other children and from the style of discipline the teachers practised. Due to this external abuse, Taylor continued to develop his imagination, which he used to survive his then current state of affairs. As entertainment, he would often play imaginary records on an imaginary gramophone: "My repertoire of tunes and imagination was quite developed by this time".[18] But this imagination could only help so much and all and all, he was quite unhappy. Somehow, his mother "heard me calling to her out in Africa" and she made enquiries that resulted in his transfer to a school in Bath in Somerset, southwest England, where he was to live with his Aunt Doris. How Taylor's mother knew what her son was feeling is unknown. It's quite possible that it was simple intuition or inference – as said above, her son had just lost his best friend and his parents – but Taylor believed it to be something more. While it is unlikely that Taylor thought much of it as a child, in his later life he came to believe that the "call" to his mother, and her reception of it was a form of extrasensory perception (ESP). In his memoirs, referring to whether or not it was ESP that made his mother reach out to him, Taylor stated "I strongly believe it".[19]

---

[16] Ibid., 15:00.
[17] Ibid.
[18] Ibid., 18:55.
[19] Ibid., 18:55.

Bath

Taylor was fascinated by Bath. The architecture and the sense of history inspired and enamoured him. He found there "plenty of scope for a vivid imagination".[20] Aunt Doris' house in which Taylor lived was in the centre of Queen's Square - "one of John Wood's famous squares" and this provided him with his "first sense of history and architectural appreciation".[21] As well, Taylor accompanied Doris on outings into the countryside, where he saw historical places such as Tintern Abbey in the Wye Valley, "which completely captivated me and gave me an early taste of such things".[22]

As for his Aunt Doris, she was an accomplished actress, business woman, and lover of Shakespeare. She owned a company that she had started with her late husband, ran the local branch of the British Empire Shakespeare Society with a friend and fellow actress, and even operated a private school out of her home, through which she taught Taylor acting and public speaking. Doris provided a strong female figure for Taylor that helped to problematize the popular discourse on womanhood that permeated Western society. Indeed, reflecting back on seeing Doris play Portia in Shakespeare's *The Merchant of Venice*, Taylor recalled, "this was how I think I saw her triumphing over men in all directions". However, Taylor also recalled Doris as a very controlling person and having quite the temper. For example, instead of "Hugh", she wanted to call Taylor "Sandy" (short for Alexander, his middle name), simply because she preferred it. Taylor, however, despised this and after quarrelling, they settled on the name "John".[23] This domineering style of raising a child taught Taylor to internalize his feelings, rather than

---

[20] Ibid., 26:30.
[21] Ibid.
[22] Ibid., 37:50.
[23] Ibid., 32:20.

express them. But more than that, being surrounded by so many powerful women affected Taylor in the eyes of society. He became more in tune with the women he grew up around and less like the Taylor side of the family, whom he saw as being far more masculine than himself. Taylor's experience with the powerful, but nonetheless 'feminine' women who raised him created a feeling of inadequacy in him. This feeling of inadequacy, the distance of his parents, and the often domineering style of Doris caused Taylor to become "a rather withdrawn person, overly fond of teddy bears and my own company".[24] After all, teddy bears "did not complicate my life".[25]

Taylor's parents returned from Africa on a six month leave of absence in 1928. Upon their return, they found Taylor to be a very different person from the one they had left two years earlier. His mother, in particular, he believed to have been "shattered" by the "fay creature, so different from the son" she had left behind. Taylor recalled this in his memoirs with humour, laughing as he mused that "I had become rather strange, I think."[26] It is unclear how conscious of this perception Taylor would have been at that age. According to him, his parents were very patient and never showed any disappointment in him, but the expressions of inadequacy made about that time in his life while writing his memoirs suggests that he must have perceived himself at that time as a disappointment to them on some level. In these memoirs, Taylor states "I can quite see why I was the source of some disappointment and heartbreak".[27] To "quite see why" implies that he was viewing evidence that confirmed a belief he already held, so whether or not he held these feelings of inadequacy in and around 1928 when this was happening,

---
[24] Ibid.
[25] Ibid.
[26] Ibid., file 2, 1:00.
[27] Ibid., 2:55.

he nonetheless clearly obtained these beliefs when he was still young.

Feelings of inadequacy such as this often lead either to acting out in some manner or "acting in", whereby the one who feels inadequate retreats from the world to their own thoughts. This is particularly true for those with developed imaginations. This retreat into the self was spurred on by other factors as well. The most pervasive of these factors was the societal expectations of the age, which Taylor describes as follows:

> Persistence, endurance and self-denial were highly rated then and I think World War I had something to do with it. In some small way we [his generation] had to try to simulate those sacrifices [of the World War I generation] which we could never match. Duty and patriotism were likewise linked with this, but at least it helped us to cope with our broken up family life and made the best of it, as also the Depression and World War II, which was to come.[28]

Retreating inward was thus a way for Taylor to deal with the various ways in which he 'failed' to fit into what he perceived as the masculine ideal. By hiding all of his 'un-masculine' and 'socially strange' thoughts and feelings from the outside world, he could better secure himself within that system of masculinity and social conformity. As well, it served as a more personal defence mechanism as Taylor had to deal with his parents' departure yet again, just six months after they had returned and just after he had gotten to know them again: "I just had to become rather self-contained in some ways in order to survive [my parents' absence]".[29]

These feelings of distance from his parents were compounded with feelings of distance from his peers, as Taylor's Aunt Doris kept a watchful and authoritative eye on who he associated with. Taylor recalled one summer during which he began playing with a group of children who were "noisy [and] healthy", having sand fights, making paper water bombs and engaging in similar playful activities. Doris was angered by this as she

---
[28] Ibid., 2:55.
[29] Ibid.

believed Taylor was "mixing with the wrong type of children," and punished him for it.[30] Associating with "normal" children such as this was seen by Taylor's Aunt as contributing to what Taylor described as his nervous and hyper behaviour – possibly a form of what we would refer to today as attention deficit hyperactivity disorder, or perhaps a form of anxiety. To combat it, Doris would often make Taylor sit in a chair each day for 6 to 12 minutes without fidgeting.[31]

As Taylor describes her, Doris played an interesting and paradoxical part in his life. On the one hand, as seen above, she could be overbearing, harsh, and developmentally limiting, forcing Taylor into an emotionally introverted state of living within his own mind, somewhat removed from the outside world, where thought and imagination differed little, if at all from the external "reality". On the other hand, the uniqueness of her lifestyle amidst the discursive backdrop of Britain's early 20th century modernist conformity stoked the fires of Taylor's developing imagination, nurturing his curiosity in all things and his unwavering interest in all things relating to stories, tales and legends. From Doris, Taylor simultaneously became introverted and extroverted. While on the one hand, he would often retreat into or reside within his own thoughts, he would also engage with stories and imaginative expression in a very direct and extroverted way.

This tendency to favour imagination over direct "reality" was echoed in other parts of Taylor's life, such as his taste in motion pictures. Movies were always a treat as they provided a means by which to stoke and engage with his imagination and, even back then, movies helped him appreciate the importance and power of the "legends" that the movies portrayed versus the reality that they were based on. *Lawrence of Arabia* came to

---

[30] Ibid., 11:15.
[31] Ibid., 11:15.

mind on this subject as Taylor, in his memoirs, recalled the effect movies had on him. He recalled how he believed that the story told in the movie – the legend – had a value and significance all its own, regardless of the integrity of its literal truth.[32] His time in Bath thus laid the ground for Taylor's fascination with media, records and archives, as the embodiment of imagination and containers of "legends".

Despite the paradoxical duality of Taylor's personality, it was no doubt the introverted, self-conscious part of Taylor that as a boy most clearly rippled through his psyche. Returning again for a short while in around 1930, Taylor's parents placed him in St. Christopher's Preparatory School, at first as a day student, attending classes for the day and returning home in the evening. After the first year, Taylor became a boarder, no doubt reinforcing his already strong feelings of abandonment. It did not help that Taylor was considered quite odd by the conformity-seeking standards of the other students and, as is the sad fate of many introverted children whose disposition differs from that of their classmates, he was subjected to frequent bullying by the other children. Generally uninterested in sports and sometimes physically unable to participate in them due to his visual disability, Taylor had a very difficult time fitting in at St. Christopher's. The experience was not completely without value though as one of his teachers interested him in entomology, which became yet another way for him to exercise his imagination. The capture and killing of the insect specimen in order to mount it never really interested Taylor; rather, the search for and exploration and discovery of life in its natural habitat, a natural performance of evolution and creation lying in wait in everyday life, interested him much more.[33]

---

[32] Ibid., 31:00.
[33] Ibid., 21:00.

With these few exceptions, Taylor's self-confidence at this time in his life was very low. He felt entirely inadequate, not only compared to other "normal" children his age, but compared to what he believed his parents expected and wanted for him. He felt guilty, believing that his parents would not have to be in Africa if it was not for the need to support him. This feeling of guilt was exacerbated in 1932 when the effects of the Depression finally reached East Africa, putting Taylor's father out of a job once again. Despite the loss of income, Taylor's parents decided to keep him enrolled in St. Christopher's. This was done so that Taylor would have the best chance of obtaining a degree, as those without one were often the first to be laid off during the Depression. Later on, as was typical of Taylor, he comprehended his feelings of guilt about this through a story: in this case, the 1934 movie *Sorrel and Son* about a laid off First World War veteran who had to work in a menial job to support his son and subsequently died of a heart attack as a result.[34]

Feeding his sense of guilt, Taylor at this time had what seems to be an overwhelming feeling of inadequacy. The postwar Depression society's emphasis on practical, tangible skills and the discourse of masculinity that Taylor perceived that that emphasis fed into left Taylor feeling that he had nothing positive to offer due to his affinity for the imagination, which often came at the expense of the tangible world around him. This is shown by the fact that even many decades later in his memoirs, Taylor describes his 12-year-old self in rather unflattering terms, listing mostly faults which, somewhat ironically, are seen today by many in the archival field as his most defining and valuable qualities. He refers to himself as "a dreamer with a vivid imagination, but little practical application to the usual hobbies apart from stamp collecting and

---

[34] Ibid., 32:30.

entomology" and "an exasperating generalist who flitted from one thing to another, enjoying each in turn".[35] While this somewhat removed personality unquestionably helped lead to Taylor's revolutionary contributions to archival theory, they were at the time marks of shame, particularly when measured against his parents and relatives, as Taylor describes:

> Above all I had a formidable feeling of inferiority towards my parents, especially my father, who – a practical, patient and very determined engineer, a brave and successful soldier. My mother too had had a very promising career when she gave it up to get married – she was a singer. Also towards the rest of the Taylor family who were hearty, good at sports and, possessed of all the positive middle class virtues.[36]

Tynemouth

In 1933, after a year of attempting to support Taylor's enrolment in St. Christopher's despite the loss of family income, it was financially impossible and Taylor was withdrawn from the school, moving with his parents to Tynemouth to be closer to the Taylor side of the family. At this time, Tynemouth was deeply entrenched in the Depression as was Taylor's family. He and his parents lived in a single, Taylor family owned house with many other relatives, where they got by on sold jewellery and lent money. Despite their newfound poverty, his parents refused to resort to using government food stamps referred to as the dole. Fortunately, the family was never forced to compromise that as they always had enough to eat. Taylor recalls the members of his extended family as being very kind to him and he being responsive to them in return, but as he saw it, they had no shared interests. And so he often used to long to return to Bath, where he could continue to immerse himself in a culture that had more room for

---
[35] Ibid., 34:30.
[36] Ibid.

imagination.[37]

There were some means by which Taylor was able to stoke his imagination. History and the shadows it cast into the present consistently became a focal point for Taylor's imagination. His growing need to feel a sense of connection latched onto the perceived unfamiliarity of the past, so stark in contrast from the feelings of inadequacy that characterized his present. The last voyage of the *Mauritania*, for example, sailed through Tynemouth with a sense of pomp and romanticism – that of a "heroic...bygone age"[38]. The Taylor family had a personal connection to this ship as well, as Taylor's father's apprenticeship involved it and his grandfather helped build it. Taylor was so fascinated by it that he began to sketch it and read about it obsessively. He even attempted to get a job on the ship, but was unable to do so, as Taylor himself put it, "For all my romantic attachment, I did not have the practical skills, but I suppose this added to my store of historical images".[39]

This fascination with the historical and his perceived lack of practical skills were not unrelated. As mentioned above, Taylor saw the soldiers of World War I, particularly his father, as near mythological figures. This contrasted with the current financial struggles of Taylor's family and created in his mind a cognitive distortion in which he likely exaggerated the contrast between his father as he was in the present, after Taylor's birth, and that mythical image of him prior to Taylor, rendered in his mind so heroically and romantically. Taylor no doubt blamed himself for this perceived change from perfect past to struggling present. On the other hand, however, this fascination with history allowed him in a sense to live in that world before he was born, where his father was far

---
[37] Ibid., 27:45.
[38] Ibid., file 3, 0:30.
[39] Ibid., 1:00.

from struggling and was at the prime of his life, or so Taylor perceived. Thus Taylor's conception of history was a sort of emotional history that simultaneously connected and removed him from his father.

In addition to a love of history, Taylor had a number of hobbies and passions while living in Tynemouth. Music and gardening had long been a passion of his that went back to his time in Bath. While still living in Bath, Taylor would sometimes come to Tynemouth to visit his grandmother and grandfather, on his father's side. During these visits, Taylor's grandfather gave him his first taste of a gramophone and he and Taylor would often listen to records together, bonding with one another over a mutual respect for the medium.[40] Gardening was another passion that Taylor inherited from his grandparents. He often used it as a means to calm himself during the more trying periods of his life. In his memoir, he mentions it frequently, especially when he discusses negative feelings that he held: in Bath, while feeling isolated during his parents' absence,[41] and again in Tynemouth, during the worst parts of the Depression, when describing how inadequate he often felt.[42] This passion for gardening later helped to fire his passion for environmentalism as it taught him the value of life in all its forms.

The popular entertainment media became another of Taylor's passions. Reading began to interest him more and more while in Tynemouth. He read a number of authors such as Agatha Christie, Charles Dickens, Oscar Wilde, and H.G. Wells. He also could not get enough of what he described as "omnibus tales of horror, mystery and imagination," examples of which included Jules Verne and Edgar Allan Poe.[43] Radio was

---

[40] Ibid., file 1, 20:00.
[41] Ibid., file 2, 8:00.
[42] Ibid., file 4, 1:00.
[43] Ibid., file 3, 23:00.

another medium by which Taylor stoked his imagination. As was the case for most middle class families at the time, radio became an important means by which the idea of "Britons" and "Britishness" was perpetuated and reified. Broadcasts with similar news or other programs were uniting people and families who, other than being "British" on paper, may have had very little in common. Taylor adored radio, which no doubt helped to open his mind to the importance of non-textual media later in his career. Not to be left out, movies also managed to capture Taylor's imagination. Taylor had been exposed to film while in Bath, but it wasn't until 1936 that a theatre opened in Tynemouth and he was able to go regularly. He had a wide range of tastes when it came to movies, but he made special mention of the 1933 film *Cavalcade*, which, to paraphrase Taylor's words, depicted a perfect vision of middle class values, such as they were at the time and place, as well as a sentimental view of Empire.[44] Again, this romantic view of military service and British Empire would have spoken to Taylor's dual perceptions regarding his father: romanticized hero with a bright past on the one hand, struggling shadow of his former self in the present on the other.

As the Depression continued, Taylor's parents were desperate for a source of income. They tried their luck in various cheaper lotteries, football pools and contests in the hopes of winning enough money to get by on, but to no avail. After being put out of a job by the Depression, Taylor's father and mother began a new business. Originally a carpet cleaning service, this business was struggling to be profitable until an uncle of Taylor's had the idea to expand from a strictly carpet cleaning service to a full maid service, employing women on a day or half-day basis to do housework.[45] Though it is

---
[44] Ibid., 28:30.
[45] Ibid., 8:30.

hard to believe a luxury service such as this was able to take off in the necessarily frugal world of the Depression, the business started to do well. This was a double edged sword, however, as the success of his parents' enterprise left them exhausted and with little time to fully engage with Taylor. This was nothing new, of course, as his parents' time in East Africa prepared him for distant, less available parents, but its continuation only exacerbated feelings of isolation.[46]

As has been mentioned above, these feelings of isolation often led Taylor to seek means to connect with his parents, particularly to his father. In 1934, Taylor's parents made a stable enough living to move out of the extended Taylor family home and into a new apartment. A year or so after that, they were able to afford to move into a house. The move from one place to another was nothing new for Taylor, but when his parents were involved, it meant that his father's war memorabilia came out of storage, and with a new house of their own, it could be put on display. Taylor was always fond of these items – medals, handbooks, ceremonial swords and the like – as they created an intersection between the emotional, feeling based history that so enamoured Taylor, and the heroic, almost mythical perception he had of his father's service during the war, which would have created for him an emotional connection with his father that was otherwise muted.[47]

That so many of these historically generated emotional bridges between Taylor and his father were grounded in romanticized ideas of military service was no coincidence. Taylor's own feelings of inadequacy when compared to his father were largely based on his own conceptions of masculinity and while masculinity can be

---

[46] Ibid., 15:00.
[47] Ibid., 23:00.

expressed and presented in many ways, dutiful military service would have been particularly relevant as the First World War's legacy was still so present in Taylor's life. It is no wonder that Taylor was so eager to join the rank and file when war broke out with Germany in 1939.

Another contributing factor to this decision was one which affects many young people: a lack of direction. Despite the relative success of the family business, Taylor's parents still struggled to pay for his schooling. His abilities in school were adequate, but he never truly excelled at anything, and those subjects in which he struggled – other languages and mathematics – held him back considerably. While he managed to pass his school certificate, he failed his articulation exam and had to get help from his Aunt Hilda and from costly mathematics tutors. He finally passed in 1936. As he already felt like a financial burden to his struggling parents, the idea of costing them even more money due to what must have seemed from his perspective to be a personal failure, this would have been quite demoralizing. In addition to this, after finally finishing school, Taylor was not quite sure what to do with himself. His self-styled role as the exasperating generalist did not lend itself well to a society that was increasingly focused on specialization. Due to his knack for drawing, he attempted an architectural apprenticeship, but failed. He also took the Customs and Excise exams, which required schooling in chemistry, which he took as a correspondence course from Metropolitan College in 1937. In January 1939, upon the course's completion, Taylor wrote the Customs and Excise exams, but again failed. It was not just professionally that Taylor struggled. He tried to learn carpentry and was sent by his parents to dance classes and classes to learn how to play bridge, both attempts to help him better acclimatize to social situations. He was, however, good at none of the above.[48] There is no question that these failures once again reinforced his feelings of inferiority, which fueled his paradoxical feelings of isolation from and perceived over-reliance on his parents, particularly his father. It was at this point, however, that the Second World War intervened and changed all that.

As has been previously mentioned, Taylor had a fascination with military symbolism and with the institution as a whole in the abstract. It was never the killing or the actual warfare that Taylor was enamoured by. Rather, the military was a vessel through which, in Taylor's eyes, purpose, duty and worth could be obtained for all to see, his father included. This can be seen in the way he interacted with the military and military symbolism as a discursive entity. These interactions included his fascination with his father's war memorabilia, as symbolic rather than practical, his love of the movie *Cavalcade*, as a transmitter of values rather than scenes of battle, as outlined above, and his view of his father as a quasi-mythological, heroic figure whose service made him virtually unreachable in Taylor's mind. Indeed, in many ways, his reverence for military symbolism was one of the few ways that Taylor felt connected to his father. When Tynemouth Castle burned down in 1938, for example, Taylor was rather distraught as his father had been stationed there during the First World War. Taylor felt a connection to it.[49] This symbolism was thus very important to Taylor, to the point where even the way he played with toy soldiers was steeped in it. Many children played with toy soldiers, but unlike most, Taylor was rarely interested in playing out battles and actual warfare. Rather, he preferred to stage military parades and the like, which, by their very definition,

---

[48] Ibid., 42:20.
[49] Ibid., 9:30.

are meant to perpetuate the value of service, duty, and sacrifice.[50]

    This rather idealistic and romanticized depiction of military service, coupled with his feelings of inferiority, made military enlistment very attractive to Taylor. By 1938, when war with Germany seemed inevitable to many, Taylor was certain that he would be involved in it in some way or another.[51] That same year, he attempted to join the RAF as an aerial photographer, but his visual impairment led to their refusal. The RAF did say to Taylor, however, that he should come back if there was a war on and they would accept him. Taylor recalled this event rather nonchalantly, "I did and they did".[52] When Britain declared war on September 3, 1939, Taylor got on his bicycle and rode up to the RAF recruitment office that same day. He chose the RAF largely because he wanted to distance himself from his father in the army. If he were in the army with his father, he would once again be directly in his shadow, unable to find himself on his own terms and stand up in his own name. Service in the RAF would allow him to follow in his father's path to near mythology, at least in Taylor's eyes, prove himself of value, and to be able to look his father in the eye as an equal.

The War Years

    The war – or rather, more specifically, being in the RAF – had a profound effect on Taylor. It was through his military service, where collegiality and strong social bonds become necessary for survival, that he was able to discover himself as an independent person, one who had moved out from his father's shadow and had begun to take stock of his own value and abilities. As Taylor says in his memoir, joining the RAF was "a totally new experience for us all...this was the ebb I had been waiting for without knowing it,

---

[50] Ibid., 23:00.
[51] Ibid., file 4, 9:30.
[52] Ibid., file 3, 42:20.

that would lead on to Oxford, archives, marriage, family, and, finally, Canada, in years to come."[53]

Taylor began his training at an RAF base in Cardington, Bedfordshire in central England. Here, he and other new recruits were given the basic training they would require for service in the RAF, along with their uniforms and supplies. The training was primarily training in discipline, as Taylor's memories of that place emphasize the foul mouths of corporals and other non-commissioned officers (NCOs), weekly kit inspections, the daily making of beds and other such tasks meant to instil the importance of duty and the chain of command.[54] Unlike many other recruits, the discipline did not bother Taylor that much as he was used to his disciplinarian aunt, parents, and teachers as a child and expected life to be so. It was also fortunate that the flight sergeant instructing his unit of recruits was not overbearing in his drill methodology. Still, as can be expected with any recruit, Taylor did not avoid punishments entirely. He remembered one time in which he overstayed his Christmas leave by a day when trying to meet his holiday familial responsibilities, without obtaining the proper documentation. For this he was locked in the guard house for a time as punishment.[55] Despite believing that the RAF sometimes pushed discipline too far, Taylor recalled that as a whole it was important as a means of creating a sense of solidarity.[56] This sense of solidarity was important to Taylor as it was the first time he ever felt as though he fit in. While he admitted that he was often seen as odd by his fellow recruits and was treated by them as someone whose

---

[53] Ibid., file 4, 11:00.
[54] Ibid.,12:30.
[55] Ibid., 15:00.
[56] Ibid., 13:50.

sheltered innocence needed protecting,[57] he was nonetheless a part of the group, experiencing the same challenges and emotions that the others were experiencing. As a result of this, he now not only had a "worthwhile" job, something that he struggled so hard with before the war, but also a task that so many other "normal" people his age were a part of. This gave him confidence and a feeling of belonging that he had lacked and struggled to find previously.[58]

It wasn't long after this that Taylor was moved to nearby Upwood, Huntingdonshire (now Cambridgeshire). There the new recruits began to specialize in their roles in the RAF. For Taylor, this meant the beginning of his training as a wireless operator in the use of Morse code. Taylor struggled to remember his reasons for choosing to train as a wireless operator – being a pilot or gunner was unlikely due to his visual impairment -- and there was perhaps a fair number of vacant wireless operator positions available. He recalls that this choice would influence his future far more than he was aware of at the time.[59] While he had long been enamoured with radio, films, and other forms of mass communication, it was in the RAF that he was forced through learning Morse code to think in fundamental ways about these non-textual forms of recorded communication. Later in life, while writing and recording his memoirs, Taylor understood this:

> I found it very satisfying when I finally got hold of it and all those signals in space from which the right one had to be selected rather appealed to my romantic nature. Here was a completely non-verbal, non-literate language with nothing but dots, dashes, and spaces, long before the computers – on, off, in the age of [Marshall] McLuhan. This would be my professional language for the next five years and it probably had some effect on my future interest in   mass

---

[57] Ibid., 14:50.
[58] Ibid., 15:30.
[59] Ibid., 19:10.

communication.⁶⁰

This opportunity to see this sort of communication reduced to its most basic form was instrumental in helping Taylor understand – through Marshall McLuhan – how communication worked on the larger scale. Within the Taylor Family Archive in Nova Scotia, a letter from Taylor's father exists, written in late 1939, that along with some encouraging words of wisdom, explains this process of understanding the pieces to understand the whole. The letter states:

> Just one word of advice and that is, wherever you have to learn, whether drill, guns, or pilotry, find out all about the inside of things and don't be content with just knowing how to fire a gun or how to drive an aeroplane. Be content when you can take them all to bits, put the bits in a bag and build them again blindfolded.⁶¹

This sort of logic is no surprise given that Taylor's father was an engineer, and it is unknown whether or not Taylor consciously put this methodology in action because of his father's advice, but it is undeniable that in his future career as an archivist, Taylor's ability to see the smallest, most fundamental pieces of the profession and how they fit together as a whole, to be built and rebuilt, was one of his greatest strengths. Learning Morse code, and the sort of thinking that his father encouraged, certainly played a part in developing this ability.

In the summer of 1940, those choosing to be wireless operators were posted to Number 2 Electrical and Wireless School in Yatesbury, near Calne, Wiltshire, in southwest England, not too far from Bath. This Wireless School was a large camp of huts in which the trainees learned to employ Morse code at 18 words a minute, a rate that would be considered slow by many veteran professionals, but which took Taylor and the

---

⁶⁰ Ibid.
⁶¹ NSA, Taylor Family Archive, MG 1, Vol. 2968, FD 4, Hugh Taylor Sr. to Hugh Taylor Jr., May 12, 1939.

other wireless recruits about six months to achieve.[62] Despite the hot weather that summer and often frustrating work with communication technology that would be considered very antiquated by[63] today's standards, Taylor found his time at Yatesbury to be quite enjoyable. When they were not being instructed, the recruits were free to socialize, listen to the radio and otherwise pass the time. Being so close to Bath, Taylor even made some excursions to see Doris with a fellow wireless recruit that he had befriended while in Upwood. By this time, Doris had become a "super Patriot, fire eating, air raid warden" who would later go on to play a significant part in the Baedeker raids of 1942 in which German bombers targeted places of historical and cultural significance throughout the UK.[64]

While Taylor had joined the RAF partly to step out from the shadow of his father, there were times when he was still unable to outrun it. In June of 1940, his father insisted that Taylor try for a commission, despite his lack of experience. His father pulled some strings and set up a meeting for his son. Taylor was not happy about this as he considered it meddling, and his commanding officer would have agreed, as the commission interview took place without his approval. Taylor is certain that his commanding officer would have laughed him out of his office had he asked and thus felt like a "complete idiot" when the interviewers told him that they wouldn't even consider it without his commanding officer's approval.[65]

Despite this, by the end of the summer Taylor successfully completed the Yatesbury training and the Air Ministry decided that he should be trained as a navigator

---

[62] JSJT, file 4, 17:20.
[63] Ibid., 25:00.
[64] Ibid., 20:00.
[65] Ibid., 22:00.

to act both as navigator and wireless operator on Beaufighters in the Middle East. Before he was placed in a navigation training program, however, he was restationed to an RAF base at Silloth, in Cumbria, North England. This base was used as a training facility for Hudson Bombers and Taylor was put to work servicing their radios. This was just temporary, however, as not long afterwards, he went on to Prestwick, in Scotland, were he was to be trained as a navigator. Taylor found in Prestwick a heavy air of elitism, as those training there had just recently been recruited, but were promoted to sergeant rather quickly and were suddenly covered with symbolic pieces of clothing that showed it. Taylor, however, struggled with navigation until it was decided that he lacked what it took to be a navigator and he was moved back down the ranks to his AC 2 position.

There was a silver lining to this demotion, however, as Taylor was stationed in Oban, on Scotland's west coast, facing the Scottish Isles. Oban was a ground station under coastal command, meant for ships and submarines, but its relative isolation and natural beauty was considered "paradise" by Taylor and he enjoyed his time there. Despite this, Taylor was determined to move upward in the RAF and after passing a radio exam, he was once again promoted to AC 1. At this point, he decided to apply for a gunnery course as it was the standard next step for wireless operators to advance. Taylor was moved to an air gunnery school in Pembrey, Wales to undergo training. Taylor's visual disability almost held him back again. In his papers can be found an RAF "Observers and Air Gunners Flying Log Book", which has the results of his gunnery tests written inside. While he was praised for being "above average" on the principles of gunnery, his inability to apply them in field tests – certainly due to his problems with vision – led to failing grades. However, the RAF was at this time not in a position to turn down gunners, so he was allowed to take the test again, eventually passing once they made it considerably easier than normal for him.[66]

Taylor was placed in a special group called "38 Group", which was created specifically to tow gliders that could contain paratroopers, propaganda leaflets encouraging European resistance, supplies, or even special agents. In December 1941, Taylor became part of 38 Group's Squadron 297, which was stationed in Netheravon, again in Wiltshire, where he had been transferred after completing his gunnery training. It was common practice that pilots picked their crews and that crews stayed together for relatively long periods of time. Taylor became the wireless operator for a pilot by the name of Allan Milson, with Cecil Haymond, who was a librarian before the war, as their navigator. Training flights began in February 1942, and Taylor spent about eight months in training exercises, acting as the wireless operator of an Armstrong Whitworth Whitley Bomber, a rather outdated aircraft, even then, dropping paratroopers with their supplies. In May 1942, Taylor's pilot was transferred to become squadron leader and flight commander of Squadron 296, where Taylor followed him. While Taylor intellectually understood how dangerous being in the RAF could be, it wasn't until an accident occurred in July 1941, when the plane he was in crashed on takeoff, killing a young recruit in the plane's nose, that Taylor truly felt the looming possibility of dying while in the service. He never flew as carefree after that event as he had before.[67]

Taylor was a competent enough wireless operator that he often flew with wing commanders, which could be seen as prestigious, but which also meant that he was under more scrutiny from the wing commanders than he was when flying with others. This also

---

[66] NSA, Taylor Family Archive, MG 1, Vol. 2968, FD 2, Observers and Air Gunnery Flying Log Book, c.1940s.
[67] JSJT, file 4, 31:00.

meant that Taylor's crew tended to be one with which new methods or manoeuvres were first tested. His first operation was on October 10, 1942, in which his crew was to tow a glider carrying propaganda leaflets into Nazi occupied France. These missions could be particularly dangerous as it all depended on the accuracy of the navigator and on the integrity and safety of the drop zones below, where they would usually be guided by the flashing signal of a resistance operative on the ground. If the drop zones had been compromised, however, the planes became easy targets. There was one situation, for example, where the drop zone prepared for Taylor's crew was near a German air base. Another time, Taylor recalled his pilot flying into a storm and then nearly crashing while trying to compensate for the turbulence. Another real danger were German anti aircraft guns armed with blue search lights. While these glider runs were certainly less chaotic and dangerous compared to bombing runs, the planes they were using were woefully out of date and very low to the ground, making it difficult to take evasive action once things did become dangerous. And things could change for the worst within the blink of an eye. On returning from one operation, Taylor recalls that they were nearly fired upon by their own British anti air defences. The plane had gotten caught in the London Balloon Barrage, an expanse of steel cables to intercept low flying enemy planes, and had it not been for a search light operator recognizing them as friendly, they likely would have been fired upon.[68]

Between operations, Taylor was rather enjoying life in the RAF. He was now stationed at Hurn, Hampshire in southern England, and it was here that he met Aileen Thompson, or "Tommy", as she was known. She was an artist and amateur violinist who was working for the RAF as a sort of visual designer, designing emblems, crests and the

---
[68] Ibid., 41:00.

like. Unlike most, she shared many of Taylor's tastes, including paintings and classical music. Thompson was eight years older than Taylor, which wasn't thought highly of at the time, but Taylor was fond of her nonetheless, and she even gave him her graduating painting. Despite their affection for one another, their relationship never went anywhere and she eventually went back to teaching art, which she hated, before moving to Australia for work. She clearly meant something to Taylor though as he kept her letters right up until the time that he met his wife, Daphne.[69] In addition to this, Taylor finally managed to receive his commission.

In December 1942, it was decided that Squadron 296 would head for North Africa to assist in the planned invasion of Sicily. It was also at this time that Taylor became the wireless operator for Sydney Horne, an Australian pilot whom Taylor regarded as a philistine and who regarded Taylor's love of art and classical music to be unmasculine. Both managed to get along, however as they respected one another's abilities. On the opposite end of the spectrum, David Warner, Taylor's new navigator, was much closer to Taylor himself: he aspired to be a writer and he and Taylor remained friends for a long time after the war. Despite Taylor's differences with Horne, it was often Warner and Horne who would argue, requiring Taylor to step in as the peacekeeper. Rounding out the crew was Jackie Jones, a former butcher who acted as the crew's gunner. Taylor remained with this crew until the end of the war.

With his new crew, Taylor flew off to Gibraltar in the new Albermarle planes that Group 38 had started using. The voyage was far from peaceful, however, as the plane had engine trouble and was forced to fly very slowly down the Spanish coast, leaving the plane rather exposed. The crew contemplated cutting across Spain, but was afraid of

---

[69] Ibid., file 5, 1:00.

ending up in a Spanish prisoner of war camp if they crashed, so remained on their course, crawling onward to their destination. From there, they flew to Frouha, Algeria and then, three weeks later, to a mud airstrip outside of Kairouan in Tunisia. This was Taylor's home during his stay in North Africa and he had nothing but wonderful things to say about it. This exposure to a different culture, even by way of the imperialist presence of the British military, helped Taylor to take stock of cultural variations and to think about the assumptions that he had inherited as a white, middle-class British male. It is here that he began to challenge himself to think outside the box, as will be seen in more detail in chapter 3.

On July 9, 1943, the Allied invasion of Sicily began. Taylor's crew was responsible for towing an American Waco glider containing General George F. Hopkinson. The operation was not very well executed, however, and the Royal Navy began to fire on the Allied planes by mistake. Luckily, Taylor's crew survived this unscathed, and in the days that followed, dropped several more groups of paratroops into Sicily. The most danger Taylor's crew was in actually occurred on their way back to England on October 23, 1943, when one of the engines had a cracked cylinder and their plane began dropping in altitude. It was Taylor that suggested they change to auxiliary power, and by doing this, the plane managed to limp back home. Taylor regarded this as a "personal miracle".[70] During the invasion of Normandy on June 6, 1944, Taylor's crew flew in a single glider, but otherwise did not take part. On September 18, 1944, Taylor's last operation took place, in which his crew landed a glider in the Netherlands. Taylor had completed 29 operations, which was considered two and a half tours and he was thus not required to take part in the ongoing conflict with Japan. For Taylor, the Second

---

[70] Ibid., 14:45.

World War had ended and he was happy to leave.[71]

Postwar

As already mentioned, Taylor lived and breathed history on a daily basis. It stoked his imagination. His time in Bath had given Taylor a sense of place and period, while the shadow of World War I that so clearly affected the lives of everyone in Britain during his formative childhood years. While he learned little history at St. Christopher's, aside from the memorization of dates, a particularly well-spoken teacher in Tynemouth School had helped make 19th century English political history a fascinating subject for Taylor. Though he would have continued to study history prior to the war, if his parents had been able to afford to keep him in school, it was the war itself that led Taylor to pursue it: "Increasing reality of the past in the present became joined to a growing desire to get into some kind of constructive study or activity as making some amends for the destruction of war."[72]

Taylor was hoping to study at Oxford as it was the main centre for historical study in Britain at the time. In the meantime, however, he began to teach history for the RAF and to take correspondence courses from the University of London in order to pass the Intermediate Arts Exam. In addition to this, he also took courses at Barton Hall in Lancashire and at another institution near Manchester. This continued until January, 1946, when he was officially demobilized, completing 6 years of service. Upon returning home to Tynemouth, Taylor found his parents' business flourishing. Over the next few months, he studied for the Oxford Wolsey Hall inter-arts examination. He also suffered from what he called "nervous experiences" which he had to work out of his system,

---

[71] Ibid., 19:00.
[72] Ibid., 27:30.

possibly a type of post-traumatic stress disorder from the war.[73] Nonetheless, he applied to every university in England and accepted an offer of admission from Keble College, Oxford, providing he passed the inter-arts exam, which he did later that year.

It was at Oxford that he allowed his imagination to soar and, after falling into it rather by chance, decided to funnel this imagination towards the field of archival studies. This would lead him to Canada, which would lead him to Marshall McLuhan, which would lead to the development or, perhaps more accurately, the discovery of Taylor's unique and revelatory way of looking at archives. For now, we are able to see Taylor as he emerged from a rather typical middle-class English boyhood as a lonely, but endlessly curious introvert, latching on to symbolism and imaginative realms of waking dreamscapes in order to withstand the isolation he felt amidst the outside world. We saw him ill at ease with his place in the world, his very value as a human being questioned from within by his perceived inability to live up to his own ideas of masculinity and specialized, productive modern citizenship. We saw him shift from this dreamer to one bent on bettering himself in the eyes of others through the romanticized discourse of military service, as he perceived it, his always strong imagination funnelled towards the ideals of this service. And finally, we saw him, through the chaos and socialization of war and military service, arise as a man who sought to embrace his imagination and expand it on a professional level, determined to attend Oxford and see where that imagination would take him. It took him, of course, to archives.

---

[73] Ibid., 24:50.

Chapter Two: From Oxford to Canada: The Making of an Archivist, 1946-1993

While Taylor had grown considerably as a person, from being a shy, lonely boy to being a much more confident and self-possessed person who knew the direction he wanted his life to take, his changes were far from over. His studies in history at Oxford would inadvertently lead him to archives, which would become more than a simple passion, but something that became life affirming, and which would lead him to Canada, where his impact and influence would increase exponentially.

Oxford

Taylor began his archival career as many archivists did at the time and to some extent still do: by pursuing a history degree, more or less oblivious to what archives are, let alone considering work in one as a profession. His university odyssey began in 1946 as he embarked on a three-year honours degree at Keble College, Oxford that was considered a degree in modern history. The name of the degree was by today's standards a bit of a misnomer, as it involved only British history and went back as far as the collapse of the Roman Empire in Britain and the arrival of the Anglo-Saxons. The idea that "modernity" began with the Anglo-Saxons and that adjective-free "history" necessarily refracts through the lens of Britain and Empire was no accident. Despite the human costs of two world wars that had been perpetrated by "modern" peoples, modernist, Anglo-centric, teleological history was still the rule rather than the exception when it came to the classroom. Taylor's curriculum consisted primarily of the political and constitutional history of Great Britain.[1]

Despite this rather limiting, Whiggish historical regimen, Taylor found inspiration and ways through which to develop his creative side. One example took the form of a

---

[1] JSJT, file 5, 31:00.

tutor named J.S. Bromley, who tutored Taylor on 18th and 19th century history and, according to Taylor, was sensitive and took a deep and invested interest in the early careers of those he tutored.[2] Despite the fact that the essays Taylor submitted to Bromley were fairly straightforward and far from revolutionary in thought, he always prefaced them with argumentative pieces in which Taylor would "launch into some rather wild ideas" that he and Bromley would discuss "at length" afterwards.[3] He did this despite the fact that these pieces weren't part of the course work and as such weren't ever marked. He simply enjoyed doing them and began to develop, in his own words, a taste for the absurd. In his memoirs, Taylor would later refer to this love of absurdity as "surely the flip-side of wisdom", a comment that made him chuckle and which he referred to immediately afterwards as a rather pretentious remark.[4]

Taylor began to open up socially at Oxford. He still did not have any serious friends, but he managed to socialize a great deal, likely due to the increased confidence he felt now that he had found a direction for his life and due to his experience of camaraderie during the war. Indeed, his roommate while at Keble College was Donald Milner, a friend that Taylor had made during his service in the RAF. Taylor's new found social acumen allowed him to do things he never would have done before, such as participate in sports. His visual impairment had always made sports difficult for him, but he managed to find an athletic activity (rowing) that did not depend a great deal on his eyesight and he became quite a proficient rower. This no doubt gave him more confidence still, as he could better fit himself into his own ideals of masculinity that he so felt alienated from.

---
[2] Ibid., 40:00.
[3] Ibid.
[4] Ibid.

But Oxford did more than allow Taylor to engage in the social activities that he had previously felt left out of: it also normalized his own interests – thought, pondering, and historical study, not as an isolating process of memorization of dates and the words of long dead figures, but as an interactive, ever evolving dialogue that actively connects the past, present, and future. As Taylor put it himself in his memoirs:

> What more can I say about Oxford? A sense that education is so much more than books, but the exploration of ideas and experiences with people, all sorts of people, in a rich environment, constantly challenging to excellence, where any kind of intellectual arrogance is anathema and pretentiousness gently discouraged.[5]

While this may be a sort of romanticized view of academia as a discursive object, the fact that Taylor believed it and felt it as such shows how it was an important theatre in the transition of his thought from a static model based primarily on textuality, to a more dynamic model based on interaction and orality. This transition had enormous implications for Taylor, making him more receptive to the revolutionary philosophy of Marshall McLuhan when he finally encountered McLuhan's work in the 1960s. For now, however, Taylor had found a place that encouraged his very nature and as such he thrived.

One such way that Taylor thrived was by spearheading the revival of the Tenmantle History Society, an Oxford historical society that had dissolved during the war. In 1949, as president of the society, Taylor presided over a banquet celebrating the society's 700th meeting. The guest lecturer at this banquet was an archeologist name Christopher Hawkes, with whom Taylor debated quite vigorously about the value of myth. Interestingly enough, given Taylor's later life emphasis and promotion of myth as an important body of knowledge, he argued against its usefulness at this banquet – or

---

[5] Ibid., 38:20.

rather, cautioned against it. [6] This is in stark contrast to Taylor's later philosophy, which shows that while Oxford nurtured and expanded his thinking, it was only the beginning of his ever evolving philosophy. I will discuss this paper in more detail in the following chapter.

Taylor's religious, spiritual, and political philosophies were also nurtured at Oxford. His religious beliefs, since childhood, were steeped in "High Church" Anglicanism (with its stress on Church hierarchy and institutional authority). But even as a child Taylor found something lacking in institutional religion. While living in Bath with his Aunt Doris, herself a High Church Anglican, Taylor was required to carry the incense boat at their local church, a job he recalled disliking, finding it embarrassing and pointless, an experience that moved him away from the direction of High Church spirituality. [7]

This is not to say, however, that he opposed all aspects of the High Church. Indeed, Taylor was fascinated by church and cathedral architecture, not just aesthetically, but spiritually as well. He sought places of worship that emanated ineffable feelings of faith and peace, where architecture and faith not only came together in perfect synergy, but where they were so perfectly aligned that they were one and the same: an expression of God and evidence of God's love on earth. This can be seen in a letter Taylor sent to his mother in the early 1940s while he was in the RAF, on leave in London on his way to Westminster. He had made a visit to St. Paul's Cathedral where he described it as:

> More like a mausoleum than a church where we should worship God rejoicing...there is one little corner which does glow with real emotional appeal. It is the memorial chapel to Lord Kitchener. The little chapel was flooded with sunshine which made the marble effigy a spotless white. There it lay at the floor

---

[6] NSA, Taylor Archive, MG 1, Vol. 2955, FD 1, Hugh Taylor's speech at the Tenmantle Dinner, 1949.
[7] JSJT, file 1, 42:00.

of an altar utterly peaceful, the best memorial to a soldier I have seen.[8] Thus it can be seen that religion was a deeply personal and emotional concept for Taylor. It was not something that you did, but that you felt and engaged with. It can be seen more as a form of spirituality than a dogmatic set of rules and practices. The church, as an institution, however, was never removed from his life. He considered himself an Anglican throughout his life, even at the end of his writing career when he penned "The Archivist, the Letter, and the Spirit", perhaps the most complex and fullest expression of his spirituality (this will be discussed in more detail in the subsequent chapter).[9] In addition, he greatly enjoyed sketching churches and cathedrals, as well as nature and monuments.[10] The church as an institution, while turning Taylor off with its dogma and lack of emotion, still appealed to him for its historical and romanticized notions of religious community. It is likely for this reason that, even after moving to Canada, Taylor made sure to keep in touch with local Anglican churches and church groups, going so far as to paste a plethora of their pamphlets in one of his scrapbooks that now resides in the Nova Scotia Archives.[11]

At Oxford, Taylor nurtured this ever developing spirituality by joining various Christian groups, many of which were involved in forms of activism, the peace movement, and reconciliation with postwar Germany.[12] Taylor became intimately involved in these groups. He assisted in setting up a meeting of like-minded Christians that took place at Oxford under the direction of L.J. Collins, a Christian activist. This meeting produced two major resolutions. One concerned the participation of Christians

---

[8] NSA, Taylor Archive, MG 1, Vol. 2970, FD 1, Hugh Taylor to Enid Essex Taylor, early 1940s.
[9] Hugh A. Taylor, "The Archivist, the Letter, and the Spirit", *Archivaria* 43 (Spring 1997): 1-16.
[10] NSA, Taylor Archive, MG 1, Vol. 2955, FD 1, Various Sketches, c.1945-1950.
[11] NSA, Taylor Archive, MG 1, Vol. 2957A, FD 1, various pamphlets, c.1965.
[12] See Ibid., Vol. 2955.

in international affairs and the alignment of international affairs with Christian principles, urging Christians:

> (a) to set out to acquire clear conceptions of Christian principles and their bearing on the actual problems of society;
> (b) to play a full part (according to opportunity and ability) as working members of one or more of the national and local organizations upon whose healthy operation our public life depends;
> (c) to give support by active democratic means to the government of the day in any attempt made to maintain the application of Christian principles in national and international affairs, and to press for a policy more and more in line with these principles;
> (d) to do everything possible by example and by prayer to build up within the Churches a fellowship of Christians actively engaged in trying to work out in everyday life the social and political implications of the Gospel.[13]

The second resolution concerned reconciliation with Germany, urging Church leaders:

> (a) to formulate, for the help of H.M. Government, a positive Christian aim which would govern our nation's policy, discussions and behaviour in all matters connected with our responsibilities for Germany, including our attempts to solve the problems of the reconstitution of German family life, of the resettlement of displaced persons, and of the assurance to German people of the economic means for a proper standard of living;
> (b) to call upon Christians to see in appointments on the Continent unique opportunities of witness and reconciliation;
> (c) to consider how far and where voluntary services on the Continent would be of value, and to negotiate with H.M. Government for the maximum opportunity to implement the results of these considerations;
> (d) to continue and greatly to expand efforts to promote fellowship between the Churches in Germany and the Churches in the rest of the world.[14]

This sort of Christian activism led Taylor that same year to a conference in Heidelberg, Germany on the subject of Anglo-German reconciliation through application of Christian principles. This conference was set up when the Student Christian Movement – that Taylor was a member of – received an invitation from a similar group in Heidelberg to attend a conference on the above topic. The theme was rendered "God's Design and Man's Witness", which, using the example of reconciliation with Germany,

---

[13] L.J. Collins, "A Call to Christian Action in Public Affairs", *Theology* 50:321 (March, 1947): 92.
[14] Ibid., 92-93.

sought a return to foundational Christian principles, in opposition to

> Those countries nominally Christian [whose] indifference [is] tinged with hostility [and] though Christian viewpoints and moral standards [are] widely accepted, [they are accepted] with little sense of their origin or founding character.[15]

This, then, was a stand against intellectualized religion, practised according to custom, rather than a spiritual, emotional religion that is felt. These beliefs led Taylor and his conference counterparts to advocate for immediate reconciliation with Germany and an end to what they considered overly harsh and unjust punishments inflicted on postwar Germany. In one of his scrapbooks, Taylor included something he wrote which states the following on the subject:

> There is a deep and genuine feeling of quiet and shame for the war which has just ended; quiet that as a nation the war had been made possible; shame (and this is the stronger sentiment) that Germany should be so dishonoured in the eyes of the world...I'm not asking for cheap sentimentality towards the Germans; the war was of their making and they are suffering a given punishment, but the maintenance of peace is our problem as well as theirs.[16]

Religion was thus the bedrock of Taylor's activism, which later in life would lead him to causes such as the peace movement, nuclear disarmament, and environmentalism.

Religion and spirituality were important in another way for Taylor while at Oxford, as they led him to discover archives, albeit indirectly. According to his own account in his memoirs, Taylor did not have much exposure to archives for most of his time at Oxford as, according to him, original research was frowned upon.[17] It was not until his final year that he encountered archives, archivists, and even primary sources. He had begun writing an historical fiction account of 17th century North Shields – an account

---

[15] NSA, Taylor Archive, MG 1, Vol. 2955, FD 1, "God's Design and Man's Witness" paper by Hugh Taylor in preparation for Heidelberg, 1947.
[16] Ibid., untitled paper, 1947.
[17] JSJT, file 5, 44:00.

he later referred to as "excruciating"[18]. In conjunction with this, he had also taken a job arranging an exhibition for Christ Church North Shields' 300th anniversary, which included items from a treasure trove of primary, archival records. Prior to this, he had listed himself as moving towards a diploma in teaching, but had been hesitant about it as he had heard that the teaching style was more conservative than he would have liked. Therefore, at the time of his "excruciating" account of North Shields and the exhibition for the Christ Church's 300th anniversary, Taylor was quite open to discovering a new passion in his life, and "in deciphering the 17th century secondary hand of the first vestibule, I was hooked."[19]

In working with the original records, Taylor found the thread that wove through and connected all his interests and passions. This harkened back to his days as a Communications Officer in the RAF. In the "first churchwarden's minute and accounts written in the unfamiliar 'secretary hand' of the period", he found "a 'code' which cried out to be 'broken'".[20] This code to be broken, while not directly linked with life and death as it had been in the RAF, was nonetheless linked to it epistemologically and ontologically. "The original document with all its contextual implications, evidential power, and legal sanctity" reified the emotional, historical symbolism that Taylor was prone to getting lost in, as described in the previous chapter. These original records were for Taylor, "no matter what direction exploration in archival studies was to take me," to "remain central as the point of return."[21] The records therefore not only reified the emotionality of the past for Taylor, but also reified Taylor himself and the experiential

---

[18] Ibid., 36:40.
[19] Ibid.
[20] Hugh A. Taylor, "A Life in Archives: Retrospect and Prospect" in Cook and Dodds, eds., *Imagining Archives: Essays and Reflections by Hugh A. Taylor,* 214.
[21] Ibid.

reality in which he existed. That is to say, they not only made real his emotional connection to the past, but also, in doing so, made Taylor himself feel real, as they gave him a solid framework by which to connect with the world.

Archives in Britain

After having graduated from Oxford in 1949, Taylor pursued his new interest in records by doing research on a poor law union at the Northamptonshire Record Society in Lamport Hall. With tongue in cheek, he described the research as "a rather ruthless, harsh way of supporting the destitute in England", referring to the often gruelling mental toll that long hours of research can take.[22] Here, however, he managed to get a job from January to March 1950, working under Pat King, the society's lead archivist, and Joan Wake, the founder of the record society. To paraphrase Taylor, Wake was a very determined woman, often browbeating and aggravating the county aristocracy in pursuit of their records to preserve.[23] Taylor's tone is unclear as to whether he meant this characterization as praise or criticism, but he did seem to have a deep professional respect for Wake, as he attributed the society's success to her determination, noting that she was "the driving force behind [the] society".[24] Pat King, on the other hand, became a close friend to Taylor. It is likely that this dynamic of whirlwind passion in the form of Wake and close friendship in the form of King led Taylor to write in one of his scrapbooks "here I decided I would be an archivist".[25]

In 1950, now certain that archives were for him, Taylor enrolled in an archives program at the University of Liverpool in order to obtain a diploma in "The Study of

---

[22] JSJT, file 5, 36:40.
[23] Ibid.
[24] Ibid.
[25] NSA, Taylor Archive, MG 1, Vol. 2955, FD 1, written note, unknown date.

Records and Administration of Archives".[26] His course work followed typical conceptions of archives at the time. It was divided between learning how to administer an archives and learning how to read records. Though with courses like "Medieval Paleography, Chronology and Sphragistics", and Editing and Calendaring, the focus was strictly on written records.[27] The study of records and archiving was taught very much like a science or trade, with specific, manual-based rules that rarely if ever approached the humanities.[28] There were some instances when this type of by the book instruction was too limiting for Taylor. One professor in particular had a habit of reading directly from a textbook, never venturing from what was written on the page. Taylor found this frustrating and in a subtle attempt to poke fun at this manner of teaching, Taylor would often open the professor's book and mark the page where the lesson would start, as it was so predictable. In his memoir, Taylor says that the professor in question got the message, but doesn't elaborate on what he means by this. Presumably the professor took it as a sign to try other teaching methodologies.[29] As well, because the documents in question were so old, (often 17th century and older), the class rarely got to handle originals. These minor frustrations aside, Taylor was excited to be pursuing such an education. So set was he on pursuing archives that he paid for the education out of his own pocket rather than pursuing other careers for which the government often provided ample financial assistance. The small class size (only five students in the course), which allowed for plenty of individual interaction between professors and students, may also have been attractive to him.

---

[26] Ibid., University of Liverpool examinations, June 1951.
[27] Ibid.
[28] See, for example, Ibid., Vol. 2957, FD 1.
[29] JSJT, file 6, 3:00.

After graduating from Liverpool in 1951, Taylor interviewed for a job as the City Archivist in Leeds, West Yorkshire. The archives fell under the administration of the city's libraries. Taylor was interviewed by Fred Hutchings, the Chief Librarian at the time. Taylor and Hutchings got along famously. Hutchings had, by Taylor's account, a great sense of humour and was open to new ideas, initiatives, and ways of thinking. Taylor became very close to him.[30] They remained friends for the rest of their lives. As coincidence would have it, Taylor's rival candidate for the job was Edwin Welch, a man who would later go on to become City Archivist of Ottawa and Territorial Archivist of the Northwest Territories. Their paths would cross again in Canada.

At Leeds Taylor first encountered the seemingly irreparable rift between librarians and archivists. Both groups vied for professional power and status within the libraries. Taylor tried to avoid the often nasty politicking, and when he could, tried to foster unity and understanding. Although he was often shy and timid in his personal life, it helped that when it came to work he was "absolutely self confident as an archivist".[31]

It was in this state of mind, and with the benefit of his theatrical training in Bath, that he began giving talks and presentations on the subject of archives and archiving. His first talk was a lecture given for the City of Leeds Women's Conservative Association about the value of "rubbish", specifically, ephemera. Taylor was understandably nervous, "terrified" even, given that this was his first lecture, but he decided to see it as a theatrical production and as such, his training began to pay off. Other such lectures ran the gamut from general talks about archives to talks about county history.[32] This experience would come in handy later in his various talks and presentations at meetings of the Association

---

[30] Ibid., 12:00.
[31] Ibid., 8:30.
[32] See NSA, Taylor Archive, MG 1, Vol. 2955, FD 1, announcements and programmes, c.1950s.

of Canadian Archivists.

During his time in Leeds, Taylor began to pursue a Ph.D. His proposed thesis was titled "Organized Religion in an Industrial Society, Leeds 1740-1870"[33], and though his proposal was accepted, he abandoned the doctorate, partly because he considered himself unable to grasp what was needed to be an academic, and partly because a job opened up to run an archives department in Liverpool. He jumped at the opportunity. Given his role in redefining archival theory, it is difficult to think of Taylor as not having what it takes to succeed in academia, but it must be remembered that this was long before Taylor's exposure to Marshall McLuhan and even longer before postmodernist style of thinking that Taylor became famous for was well developed, never mind accepted in the academy. It is interesting to wonder how his life and worldview would have changed if he had pursued his Ph.D. Ironically, doing so may have diminished his intellectual development as learning within the accepted epistemological paradigm of the time could quite possibly have closed his mind to other ideas more off the beaten path. This is, of course, speculative but one does wonder how archival theory today would have been affected had he continued his studies. That said, the topic of the proposed thesis is notable as it showcases Taylor's continued interest in the church, particularly the Ecumenical movement. This will be discussed in greater detail in the following chapter.

At any rate, his Ph.D. prospects were abandoned, but his career in archives moved forward with the new position in Liverpool that he began in 1954. In his memoir, Taylor has nothing but positive things to say about Liverpool as a city of trade, cosmopolitanism, and most of all music.[34] This was when the Beatles were making headway into youth

---

[33] Ibid., "Organized Religion in an Industrial Society, Leeds 1740-1870", 1954.
[34] JSJT, file 6, 20:00.

culture in Liverpool clubs such as The Cavern. Taylor, however, was still very traditional in his musical tastes and was primarily interested in the symphony. Nonetheless, he enjoyed his time living in Liverpool.

His work as an archivist for the Liverpool Public Libraries, however, was far from happy. Unlike his positive experiences with Pat King in Northamptonshire and Fred Hutchings in Leeds, Taylor found in Liverpool a superior with whom he disagreed profoundly on almost every professional and personal matter. The City Librarian was George Chandler, a man who, by Taylor's account, was a workaholic with little regard for his staff's well-being. He "appeared to have no interest in life beyond his own self advancement and the expansion of the library system"[35] It was not that Chandler was incompetent – on the contrary, his skills at charming money for the libraries out of officials was, by Taylor's account, masterful. He was always seeking new and flashy projects to wow potential investors and donors, and this did lead to much needed revenue entering the library system, but the human cost of it all on the staff was, in Taylor's words, "dismal".[36] This attitude of disregard for his staff, as Taylor saw it, caused many competent people to leave for other jobs Those who remained behind only did so because they had nowhere else to go. Taylor worked as well anyone could in such trying circumstances. His days were often filled with disagreements and defending his staff amidst the office warfare. But Taylor at least felt he had learned how to operate in the workplace with someone he "opposed professionally, but who I learned to accept as a human being".[37]

Even in such a restrictive, combative environment, Taylor found ways to innovate

---

[35] Ibid., 23:00
[36] Ibid.
[37] Ibid.

and experiment. Giving lectures was part of his job and he developed one presentation in 1957 that had more in common with artistic exhibition than the traditional librarian/archival methodology of the time. It was titled "Before our Time: An Experiment in Local History". Taylor showed a series of old 3 1/4 inch by 3 1/4-inch lantern slides from the many thousands in the Libraries' collection, accompanied by a pre-recorded commentary on tape. The slides were manually changed each time a tap is heard on the tape. In doing this, Taylor sought to

> give an impression of the Liverpool community as it has changed through the centuries...there is plenty of 'straight' history to hold the passage of time together, but I have introduced plenty of contempory [sic] comment from contempory [sic] documents to try and show how people thought and acted in relation to their social environment.[38]

Each tape reel was about 80 minutes long and

> The commentary is extemporized and this means that the speech is relatively slow, giving a chance for the audience to look carefully at the slide, and is essentially conversational to try and preserve a sense of freshness. On the other hand, I have found that reading extracts from original source can be much more effective when the reader is not <u>seen</u> to grope from one book after another for his quotation. The idea is that the audience should move with the commentator and think with him at his pace.[39]

Experiments such as this show Taylor's growing belief that archives and history should not only be understood intellectually, but should also be felt emotionally, to understand them at a holistic level. However, Taylor was not happy in Liverpool. Too much of his time and effort was spent in reaction to the unreasonable demands and expectations of Chandler. Taylor desired more. Archives were not just a job for him. He began to experience

> A growing realization that the records of society – its history, its culture – and

---

[38] NSA, Taylor Archive, MG 1, Vol. 2955, FD 1, "Before our Time: An Experiment in Local History", 1957, emphasis in original.
[39] Ibid., emphasis in original.

current ways of communicating these with dramatic warmth and enthusiasm, was a good way of going about [archiving], stimulated by a struggling belief in the nature of life for a fully rounded person in my chosen field, in contrast to the narrow path of bookishness and ruthless manipulation which George Chandler seemed to me to represent.[40]

This enmeshing of archiving, communication, and personal growth and meaning was a significant step in the development of Taylor's worldview. In the same way that military life and symbolism had validated Taylor's worth in his own eyes and connected him to his father, his proficiency at archiving enhanced his self-worth and confidence. It connected him to the world around him, past, present, and future, where once he had felt isolated. This can be seen in the fact that despite being a lifelong friend of Pat King and Fred Hutchings, Taylor admits in his memoirs that he was "quite ambitious and aggressive professionally, but rarely got alongside people at a deeper level, although I think I appeared to do so".[41] Archives had become a portal by which Taylor could connect with the world and feel that deeper, spiritual sense of belonging that he had always sought. It was for this reason that Taylor felt he had to leave his position in Liverpool and considered professional options as far afield as Fiji. He ended up finding a local position, however, in 1958, when he was appointed the first County Archivist of Northumberland. In an uncharacteristic manner, Taylor lambasted Chandler in his going away speech, accusing him of treating books and records as commodities in a warehouse rather than the emotionally charged cultural and personal objects that Taylor considered them to be and of treating his staff in a similarly dehumanizing manner.[42]

Before moving to his new position, however, Taylor experienced a positive upheaval in his personal life. Taylor's romantic life receives little mention, either in the

---

[40] JSJT, file 6, 34:00.
[41] Ibid., 10:00.
[42] Ibid., 34:00.

Taylor Family Archive in Nova Scotia, or his memoirs. The latter only contains a short list of women whom Taylor shared romantic moments with before meeting his wife, followed by a rather general statement that he hopes their lives led them to happiness.[43] Taylor met Daphne Johnson while living in Liverpool in 1958. They married and he spent the rest of his life with her. Poetically enough, Taylor's other great life interest besides archives (religion) brought them together. In Liverpool, Taylor had reluctantly taken on the job of Secretary of the Local Council of Churches. He was not as confident in matters of religion as he was in archives, so this position was difficult for him. His old shyness returned. But evidently not entirely! He met Daphne at the British Council of Churches Conference in Swanwick, Derbyshire in 1958. Taylor attended as Secretary of the Local Council of Churches and Daphne as secretary to the Reverend Kenneth Slack, who was the General Secretary of the British Council of Churches. Taylor does not specify how they got to know each other and on what ideas they connected, but given that it was a religious conference and the both of them were in favour of ecumenical Christianity, it is likely that that had something to do with it. They were married on January 3 1959 and on November 13th of that year their first daughter Madeline was born. They chose Paris for their honeymoon and Taylor, never one to miss an opportunity to insert archives into a seemingly unrelated event, made certain to take ample photographs of the Archives nationales.

Daphne had a profound impact on Taylor's life and outlook. While Taylor had always been socially conscious, Daphne was the true activist, engaged in everything from helping refugees to nuclear disarmament and environmentalism.[44] These issues would

---

[43] Ibid., 29:00.
[44] Daphne Taylor, phone interview by author, October 13, 2014.

influence Taylor on a personal level, as well as professionally, as he began to incorporate their lessons and values into archives, theoretically and practically. But more immediately, in Daphne, Taylor found someone to engage with, to connect with, and to share experiences with, mollifying much of the loneliness he was so prone to experience. Despite this, their living situation early in their marriage was far from easy. After receiving his appointment in Northumberland, Taylor's parents bought a house next to their home in Tynemouth for him to live in, which Taylor had agreed to do before he met Daphne. Lacking the financial means to buy a house of their own, he and Daphne had no choice but to live in this house after they were married. This was especially hard on Daphne because Taylor's mother was prone to anxiety and required a lot of attention, support that often fell to Daphne to provide while Taylor was at work. The situation was exacerbated in 1960 when Taylor's father died. Taylor's mother's anxiety became worse, and, once again, Daphne had to bear the brunt of the fallout. She wasn't entirely burdened, however, as she continued to engage in activist causes through church groups and women's associations.

    Taylor's professional life at the Northumberland County Records Office, however, was going very well for him. As he was the first to hold the position, he had to start the archives from scratch, which proved both challenging and rewarding and would later help him with his work in Canada. Given Taylor's family connection to Northumberland, and the time that he spent in the county as a child, he thought that the chance to start an archives on his "home ground" was "an archivist's dream."[45]

    Northumberland's multifaceted history provided Taylor with a treasure trove of varied sources to engage with. Spanning "the Roman occupation, Anglo Saxons and

---

[45] Taylor, "A Life in Archives: Retrospect and Prospect", 214.

Danes, mediaeval [sic] settlements, the coal trade, the wool trade, and the agricultural and industrial revolutions", Northumberland historical records appealed to Taylor's generalist sensibilities. At the same time, Taylor had developed a respect for regional, specialist historical knowledge that would see him through his career in various provincial archives in Canada. He began to develop this appreciation in his first job in Northamptonshire, and it grew with each new location in which he engaged historically and emotionally (one and the same for Taylor). Taylor was so excited about the history of Northumberland that he even attempted to install the archives in an old castle manor, believing that its architecture would be the perfect way to help researchers to feel the history around them, as he often felt it through architecture, particularly that of churches and cathedrals. This was thought possible as the wealthy aristocrat who owned the manor was considering donating it to Taylor's newly established county archives, but at the last minute, decided against it. Upon reflection, Taylor felt that had this succeeded, it may not have been as well thought out as he had first believed. The location would be difficult for many users to get to. He chalked it up to "one of those wonderful dreams that I sometimes have, and they don't always come off".[46] Despite this set back, Taylor immensely enjoyed his time as County Archivist of Northumberland. Even long after leaving for Canada, he remained interested in the affairs of the county archives. Within his family fonds at the Nova Scotia Archives are annual reports for the Northumberland County Archives through to 1978.[47] Taylor clearly remained interested in his old post (also his "home" post) well after he left. Despite this obvious love for Northumberland, Taylor's fate as an archivist and theorist would take him several thousand miles to the west to Canada.

---

[46] JSJT, file 6, 40:00.
[47] NSA, Taylor Archive, MG 1, Vol. 2973, FD 1, R.M. Gard to Hugh A. Taylor, 1978.

Canada

When Taylor was working in Liverpool, George Chandler, despite all the frustration he caused him, predicted that for Taylor to excel as an archivist, he would have to leave Britain.[48] As it turns out, for all his insularity and disregard for his staff, Chandler was right about Taylor, as, despite all the good work he had done in Britain, it was in Canada that Taylor changed the face of archival theory, both in thought and in deed. Taylor's reasons for leaving Britain for Canada were fairly mundane: in Taylor's own words, with a purposefully high inflected tone and staccato enunciation of each word so as to express the humorous universality of the situation: "we were slowly going broke."[49] At this point, in 1965, Taylor had three daughters under seven to support and, despite his success as the Northumberland County Archivist, had few prospects for promotion. The field was still relatively new and full of young people who were not going to vacate their positions soon. Also, the Tynemouth air played havoc on the lungs of Daphne and Mary, their second daughter, both of whom suffered from asthma.

As for why Canada, Daphne had spent a few years living in there in the 1950s and, perhaps more importantly, there were better paying archival positions there. In 1963 Taylor had applied for one at the University of Toronto and was made an offer, but ultimately rejected it as he claimed that his financial situation had improved since he had applied and that he believed a Canadian would be better suited to fill that position.[50] This seems an odd statement given that two years later, Taylor would take a job establishing the Provincial Archives in Alberta, a task that arguably is more suited to a Canadian, if

---

[48] Taylor, "A Life in Archives: Retrospect and Prospect", 216.
[49] JSJT, file 6, 43:00.
[50] NSA, Taylor Archive, MG 1, Vol. 2956, FD 1, Hugh A. Taylor to unknown University of Toronto employee, 1963.

such arguments of ethnicity are to be made at all. It is also odd given that Taylor's memoirs so matter-of-factly refers to their financial situation as dire, without any mention of improving prospects in 1963, let alone those same prospects falling again two years later. In all likelihood, the Taylors were simply reluctant to move in 1963, but were finally compelled to do so in 1965.

In 1965 Taylor learned of a call for candidates to apply to become the first Provincial Archivist of Alberta. For the reasons mentioned above, Taylor applied. Due to the distance between Taylor and Alberta, much of the interview process was done by letter. Taylor was made an offer and after much discussion with Daphne, the two of them decided that Taylor should accept and at 45 years of age, he left Britain on the R.M.S. *Carinthia* and landed in Montreal. As always, Taylor was conscious of the need to feel the history around him rather than simply understanding it intellectually. He thus chose to travel by boat and train rather than by plane. He described his reasoning in a 1967 paper he gave at a meeting of the Archives Section of the Canadian Historical Association:

> As immigrants, we decided to enter Alberta by the traditional route from Europe, that is by sea and railway, and for us as for so many thousands of others, Quebec became the gateway to Canada. I think this is an important historical experience, for there is a danger that those who travel by air may feel that they are landing in some distant territory which is out of context with its surroundings, an island in a sea of land. We were conscious of Quebec as a most ancient and beautiful gateway to Canada, and we will not forget our very warm welcome on the threshold by the Immigration authorities. In our journey across Canada, we soon appreciated that there was an historical, as well as physical distance to be covered.[51]

As had been developing for quite some time, Taylor's conceptualization of history was an experiential and emotional one whereby history had to be felt and internalized to be truly

---

[51] Hugh A. Taylor, "Archives in Britain and Canada – Impressions of an Immigrant", The *Canadian Archivist* (1969): 22.

understood. With this open-minded attitude, and after being congratulated on his new post in Alberta and personally shown around the Public Archives of Canada in Ottawa by W. Kaye Lamb, then Dominion Archivist[52], he arrived at the Provincial Archives of Alberta.

The Provincial Archives of Alberta had begun unofficially as early as 1906 when the Provincial Library was created and began taking in archival records from the private sector. In 1962 the Museums Branch in the Department of the Provincial Secretary was created in order to facilitate the creation of both a Provincial Archives and a Provincial Museum, with government records beginning to be collected in 1963.[53] Upon Taylor's arrival, a new museum and archives building was being constructed at Government House in Glenora, Edmonton, while the government collections were being transferred from the Legislative Library to Beaver House, a short distance away. In Alberta, Taylor experienced an archival situation quite different from that which he was used to in Britain. In Canada, needs of historians were the chief concern of archivists, who should ideally be historians themselves. This is quite far removed from the British context in which leading archivists such as Hilary Jenkinson maintained that archivists ought not to be historians. Archivists should act as impartial custodians rather than be concerned about the records' use as "the raw material of history", as Taylor himself worded it.[54]

In addition, the types of records Taylor was now dealing with had changed dramatically. No longer was he working with centuries-old written sources. The earliest records Taylor now had were from the settler-colonial apparatus that had been forcibly

---

[52] NSA, Taylor Archive, MG 1, Vol. 2985, FD 4, K. Lamb to Hugh A. Taylor, August 19, 1965.
[53] "Our History", Provincial Archives of Alberta Website, http://culture.alberta.ca/paa/about/ourhistory.aspx, last accessed April 18, 2016.
[54] Taylor, "Archives in Britain and Canada – Impressions of an Immigrant", 22.

established in the late 1800s. In reflecting on this, Taylor expressed little longing for a return to older records. He saw the difference in relative terms. There was "just as much excitement in locating a cache of documents 80 years old in Alberta as there is of locating a box of medieval charters 800 years old in England".[55] In fact, these more recent records were in some ways even more interesting for Taylor as their relative youth required that attention be paid not just to their archival value, but to their value as semi-active records that still required a degree of records management to be in place, something which could not be said for the very old documents that Taylor had worked with back in Britain.

Lastly and most important, the move to Alberta exposed Taylor to different types of records that he had not been exposed to much to this point in his career. In particular, photographs, which Taylor referred to as one of "the great glories of Canadian archives", the like of which was not found in British archives at the time.[56] The collections he was referring to were those of pioneers of the Canadian Prairies who were so fond of taking photographs of the land's alleged emptiness, followed by photographs of their development of the land.

This exposure to photographs was but one new experience the Canadian scene gave Taylor. As the Alberta archives was administratively part of the museum, Taylor was not only exposed to the records that concerned archivists at the time, but also to a plethora of museum artifacts. The distinction between them began to blur in Taylor's mind. He "began to take the artifactual base of records less for granted. They could be seen as part of our material culture over against the constant presence of native peoples

---

[55] Ibid., 28.
[56] Ibid., 30.

with an oral tradition which predated us by thousands of years."[57] This emerging appreciation of traditionally "non-archival" media as having archival value and therefore being the concern of the archivist was further developed by a watershed moment in Taylor's life. In 1966 one of the Siksika (Blackfoot) First Nations of southern Alberta was looking to sell a medicine bundle to the museum. To facilitate this, Taylor arrived at the First Nation in person and witnessed and took limited part in a Sun Dance ceremony to honour the transfer of this sacred object to the care of the museum. During this ceremony, Taylor saw much that would have confused most archivists of the time, who had been trained in Western methodology with little exposure to the spirituality of the Siksikawa.

    Taylor witnessed an elder cradling the medicine bundle with such care that he felt it reminiscent of how one would cradle a baby, while other members of the First Nation experienced powerful emotions, some openly weeping. This event affected Taylor powerfully. He was moved by the deep spirituality of the ceremony and it made him see the medicine bundle, and by extension, records, in a whole new light.[58] As has been mentioned, Taylor felt that history and records had to be felt in order to truly be understood, but this ceremony went beyond simply feeling records and the historicity of the world around the participants. This was a view that directly wove personal and collective spirituality into the past, present, and future of the record itself. With such a direct link between records and spirituality, records become not just something that provided historical understanding; rather, they become the very building blocks of reality through which one experiences feelings and emotion, a concept that would, for Taylor,

---

[57] Taylor, "A Life in Archives: Retrospect and Prospect", 218.
[58] Daphne Taylor, phone interview by author, October 13, 2014.

later become associated with God. But first, Taylor had to experience the second great intellectual-cum-spiritual watershed in his life: the discovery of Marshall McLuhan.

In 1967 Taylor moved with his family once again, across the country to New Brunswick, where he became the first provincial archivist and thereby helped found yet another provincial archives. Due to New Brunswick's longer colonial history when compared to Alberta, Taylor was able to return to dealing with records that could readily be considered 'historical', although they were still a far cry from the centuries old written records he worked with in Britain. "This seems like England all over again," Taylor mused in reference to the stacks of older records held in New Brunswick attics.[59] For the short time Taylor was in New Brunswick, his purview as Archivist was immense. He had not only the Provincial Archives under his direction, but the Legislative Library and records management too. Suffice it to say, he had no shortage of work.

While in New Brunswick Taylor was also exposed to the works of Marshall McLuhan. Taylor gives two slightly different accounts of how he first encountered McLuhan. In a 1993 piece, Taylor states that he encountered McLuhan while earning some extra money as a history tutor at the University of New Brunswick,[60] and in a 2000 reflection he claims to have encountered McLuhan's *The Gutenberg Galaxy* on a reading list while taking a Canadian history course, as his knowledge of Canadian history was at that time limited.[61] In all likelihood, both accounts are probably true to some degree. It seems entirely likely that Taylor was tutoring others in history while at the same time taking a Canadian history course, exposing him to McLuhan on two fronts. Whatever the

---

[59] Taylor, "A Life in Archives: Retrospect and Prospect", 218.
[60] Ibid., 219.
[61] Hugh A. Taylor, "The Media of Record: Archives in the Wake of McLuhan" in Cook and Dodds, eds., *Imagining Archives: Essays and Reflections by Hugh A. Taylor*, 72.

case, Taylor was "absolutely bowled over by him".[62] He had a great epiphany after reading McLuhan that would inspire the rest of his career: that the forms and media of records matter just as much if not more than their content, and that typography is not an objective signifier of superior historical or evidential significance, but the fact that it is viewed as such is the result of sociocultural history that was itself driven by the mentality that Europe's use of typographic recording media created. This will be discussed in more depth in the following chapter.

Having facilitated the creation of two provincial archives, Taylor set his sites on the national stage at what was then the Public Archives of Canada. In 1967 Taylor had applied for the position of Director of what was at that time called the Historical Branch, but his application was rejected.[63] He applied a second time in 1971 and got the position. His new found appreciation for McLuhan and his emphasis on the media of record led Taylor to reorganize the Historical Branch (which he renamed the Archives Branch), creating various divisions along the lines of media type, each with significant autonomy within the confines of overarching archival principles. This division produced mixed reactions from onlookers. For many, the intellectual separation of records by medium, not to mention the physical separation of the archives staff by medium with which they focused, led to the dismantling of provenance and context.[64] Taylor understood these arguments, certainly in retrospect, and the holism he expressed intellectually towards the latter part of his career (see chapter 3) would suggest that the intellectual and conceptual division of archives by medium was never his intention. Rather, what he was attempting

---

[62] Daphne Taylor, phone interview by author, October 13, 2014.
[63] NSA, Taylor Archive, MG 1, Vol. 2985, FD 4, J.P. Moussette to Hugh A. Taylor, July 12, 1967.
[64] See Terry Cook, "The Tyranny of the Medium: A Comment on 'Total Archives'", *Archivaria* 9 (Winter 1979-80): 141-149.

to "explore the mysterious power which the media of record exerted on archivists and users alike (we too were users) and to enable the staff to join in this exploration, using all the professional skills at their command and merging with the historical context."[65] Although the media divisions Taylor created no longer exist in the same state as they were in then, the Public Archives and its future incarnations were "forever after changed as a result".[66]

During his time in Ottawa, Taylor discovered that he was "a regional person at heart"[67] and often found himself struggling to cope with the sheer vastness of Canadian geography. Indeed, he simply lacked the historical background to conceive of Canada's documentary heritage in the holistic way he felt was necessary at the national level:

> When I later moved to Ottawa and the (then) Public Archives of Canada as a branch manager, I realized quite early on that I could not fully grasp in archival terms the reality of so vast a territorial entity as Canada (a little more history would have helped!). I was much more comfortable in the Provincial Archives...[68]

In 1978 he was appointed Provincial Archivist at the then Public Archives of Nova Scotia, where he would remain until his professional retirement in 1982, at which time he and his family moved to Victoria.

During his time in Canada, Taylor's professional influence went beyond the positions he held as he was also quite involved in the activities of the Canadian (and American) archival professions and in the teaching of archival principles to a new generation of emerging archivists. Taylor's role in the creation of the Association of

---

[65] Hugh A. Taylor, "Afterword: On Reflection and Imagination", in Cook and Dodds, eds., *Imagining Archives: Essays and Reflections by Hugh A. Taylor*, 246.
[66] Cook, "Hugh A. Taylor, 1920-2005", 278.
[67] Taylor, "A Life in Archives: Retrospect and Prospect", 219-220.
[68] Taylor, "Afterword: On Reflection and Imagination", 246.

Canadian Archivists (ACA) was such that Terry Cook calls Taylor its "godfather".[69] The ACA was born out of the historic split between the Canadian Historical Association (CHA) and the archivists that had formerly been a part of it. Before 1975, the only pan-Canadian forum for archivists to meet came once a year at the annual CHA conference, as members of the Archives Section of the CHA.[70] These meetings were originally simple exchanges of the year's events from various archival institutions, but as membership grew in the 1960s and early 1970s, so too did the demand for a more formal and official gathering of archivists. This led to the creation of *The Canadian Archivist,* the Archives Section's official, if infrequently released, publication. Taylor became the journal's editor in 1969 while he was Provincial Archivist of New Brunswick and immediately began to usher in changes to the format and content of the journal in an attempt to support more philosophical submissions related to archives, as a topic of academic inquiry, or as Gordon Dodds phrased it, giving it "a bit more bite".[71] As well, Taylor sought to make the publication more inclusive of all archivists, including those in Quebec, Acadia, and the various pockets of archivists throughout the rest of Canada for whom French was their primary language. To sum up these coming changes, Taylor ended an editorial in his first issue by quoting John Archer with the words, "We are slowly moving towards a Canadian archival methodology", and adding his own addendum, "Our journey should go on record".[72]

But even with their own publication, dissent among archivists continued to brew

---

[69] Cook, "Hugh A. Taylor, 1920-2005", 279.
[70] See Terry Eastwood, "Attempts at National Planning for Archives in Canada, 1975-1985", *The Public Historian* Vol. 8 No. 3 (Summer 1986): 74-91, for a concise history of the split between the ACA and the CHA, as well as the ACA's early activities.
[71] Gordon Dodds, "Hugh Taylor: The Far Away Archivist" in Cook and Dodds, eds., *Imagining Archives: Essays and Reflections by Hugh A. Taylor*, 8.
[72] Hugh A. Taylor, "Editorial", *The Canadian Archivist,* Vol. 1 No. 3 (1969): 3.

in the Archives Section of the CHA. In 1973, during the CHA conference in Kingston, the dissatisfaction in the Archives Section, particularly its younger members, was palpable. The idea that archives and archivists were the domain of historians had been challenged before this meeting and the newly philosophical direction in which Taylor took *The Canadian Archivist* only exacerbated this by showing that archivists had their own distinct perspective and interests. The following year saw the Committee of the Future set up with Taylor as its chair. It was to determine whether the Canadian archival profession wanted a standalone professional association for archivists. While several people were involved in this process, in particular David Rudkin, Marion Beyea, and Gordon Dodds, all of whom Taylor playfully referred to as the "Young Turks", according to Dodds, "Hugh's enthusiastic and overt support of the idea, and total confidence that it could be done" led to the committee's success, and that "it couldn't have been accomplished without Hugh Taylor's involvement and foresight".[73] In 1975 Canadian archivists formed the ACA and launched its own publication, *Archivaria,* in the following year.

Taylor also played an active role in the Society of American Archivists (SAA), as a Council member from 1973-1977, an Executive Committee member from 1976-1977, as well as in half a dozen other positions which culminated in his becoming the SAA's 34th President from 1978-1979. In addition to this, since 1963, Taylor held a membership in the North Eastern Region of the Society of Archivists in Britain, a membership he held onto long after he had emigrated. As with his belief in the ecumenical movement that sought to bridge the divide between Christian churches, Taylor sought to bridge the divides between archivists from around the world. In a piece

---

[73] Dodds, "Hugh Taylor: The Far Away Archivist", 9-10.

written in the SAA's publication, *The American Archivist,* just after becoming SAA president, Taylor expressed this desire to break down barriers with the following turn of phrase: "Assuredly we [Canadian and American archivists] have a professional border, but may it too stand undefended."[74]

After his retirement in 1982, Taylor began to focus his energies on teaching. He had long advocated for academic, post-graduate, pre-appointment university courses specifically designed to meet the increasingly complex and distinctive needs of archivists that educations in history or information and library sciences could not alone fulfill. Taylor had begun advocating for this type of education as early as 1973. He was convinced that it had to go beyond simply training archivists, as if for a trade, and instead teach a philosophically-infused archival theory that would not only convey how archival work should be done, and records understood, but also explore the reasons why.[75] In 1976 Taylor and Edwin Welch, the man whom Taylor had competed against in Leeds for the position of City Archivist, were members of the ACA Education Committee. They co-wrote a guide on what a post-graduate master's level curriculum in Archival Studies should involve.[76] This work directly influenced (though not without revision) the creation in 1981 of North America's first Master of Archival Studies program (at the University of British Columbia). The ACA's 1988 guidelines for the curricula of master's programs in Archival Studies would go on to influence the creation of a similar but still distinctive Archival Studies MA program at the University of Manitoba when it was launched in 1990. Taylor was on the ACA Education Committee that drafted the

---

[74] Hugh A. Taylor, "Focus", *The American Archivist* Vol. 42 No. 1 (January 1979), 9.
[75] Dodds, "Hugh Taylor: The Far Away Archivist", 10.
[76] See appendix in Terry Eastwood, "The Origins and Aims of the Master of Archival Studies Programme at the University of British Columbia", *Archivaria* 16 (Summer 1983): 35-52.

guidelines and took an active part in supporting these two new programs, as part-time teacher at UBC and visiting speaker at UM.[77] Taylor took on the coordination of a yearly month-long archives course that was sponsored by the then National Archives of Canada and which ran until 1993.

Although archives were certainly important in Taylor's life, he filled his free time with other passions, most notably environmental and peace activism. While Daphne rather than Taylor was *the* activist, Taylor was nonetheless a significant figure, particularly when it came to the subject of nuclear disarmament, a subject relevant both to the peace movement and to environmentalism. In 1982, along with other war veterans, Taylor helped to found the Veterans for Nuclear Disarmament Committee, the mission statement for which reads:

> We who have some knowledge of war and weapons, through our service in our country's armed forces, know in our hearts that the nuclear arms race can only end in disaster for all mankind. Mutual annihilation is no defence. It is time for us to join the growing number of former military leaders...in calling for an immediate end to the nuclear arms race...Canada has an important part to play in preventing nuclear war. We call upon our government to take initiatives towards NATO/Warsaw Pact nuclear arms reduction now.[78]

The committee expanded on this in another statement that acknowledged that everyone of good will belonged to the "peace movement" and that it was a higher priority than any other human concern or rivalry:

> Let us start by recognizing that in our efforts to prevent war between the superpowers and their allies, we are all in the peace movement. We differ profoundly in approaches, but we should respect those whose views differ from our own and we should not regard each other as dangerously irresponsible. We defend our values and our people by defending our territory, but in the last

---

[77] See The Education Committee, Association of Canadian Archivists, "Guidelines for the Development of a Two-Year Curriculum for a Master of Archival Studies Programme (December 1988)", *Archivaria* 29 (Winter 1989-1990), 128-141.
[78] NSA, Taylor Archive, MG 1, Vol. 3138, FD 1, CG Gifford to Hugh A. Taylor, April 29, 1982, emphasis in original.

analysis territory (which was itself once seized from others) may not be our most cherished possession; rather it should be the preservation of life on this planet.[79]

Taylor was deeply passionate about preserving the environment and terrestrial life. This was about something much grander and more significant than geopolitics or ideological conflict. It was about our very existence. This concern can be seen throughout much of Taylor's writings, as will be discussed in the next chapter.

In this chapter, we have seen how Taylor went from an eager history enthusiast at Oxford to an even more enthused young archivist working his way up the ranks of the British archival profession, only to find that his path led elsewhere, to Canada, where he would have two personal revelations in the form of his exposure to Indigenous conceptions of the sacredness of certain records and in the awe inspiring epiphany that he found in Marshall McLuhan. He spearheaded the creation of two provincial archives and redefined from top to bottom the structure of the then Public Archives of Canada, as well as helped found the ACA and post-graduate university archival education in Canada. But as impressive as this is, Taylor's true accomplishments and what made him a truly special individual in archival theory were his writings and the ideas contained therein. This will be discussed in detail in the following chapter.

---

[79] Ibid., Vol. 3138, FD 2, "The Defence of Canada: Is There a Middle Way?", c. 1982.

Chapter Three: The Cosmic Prophet

While Hugh Taylor's immense impact on Canada's archival community from a professional and organizational standpoint cannot be underestimated, it was through his unique and imaginative written pieces that he truly redefined the archival world, not just of Canada, but throughout the English-speaking world. Taylor was the first to make and is arguably largely responsible for the shift in archival theory from the influential views of luminaries such as Hilary Jenkinson and Theodore R. Schellenberg. They saw archives and records as static holders of objective truths, while Taylor pioneered a more postmodern approach that saw them as dynamic and powerful, both shaping and being shaped by those that created and used them as well as the archivists who handled them.[1]

It is through these writings that the world is able to glean small portions – dots of understanding, if you will – of Taylor's cosmic philosophy as it developed, a four dimensional connect-the-dots art project that spanned the entirety of space and time. But just looking at these dots of understanding in a vacuum, one by one, devoid of relational context, either from Taylor's life or even from how they relate to each other, is insufficient to truly understand them. While it is impossible to truly "know" Taylor's philosophy in the sense of being able to connect one's thoughts directly to his, one can create a sort of impressionist painting of his evolving worldview as it relates to his life and experiences. To borrow a phrase from Tom Nesmith from another context, our portrait of Taylor remains "still fuzzy, but more accurate".[2]

To have any hope of understanding Taylor's philosophy, one must remove oneself

---

[1] For a thorough review of Hilary Jenkinson's and T.R. Schellenberg's pivotal contributions to archival theory, see Terry Cook, "What is Past is Prologue: A History of Archival Ideas Since 1898", *Archivaria* 43 (Spring 1997), 17-63.

[2] Tom Nesmith, "Still Fuzzy, But More Accurate: Some Thoughts on the 'Ghosts' of Archival Theory", *Archivaria* 47 (Spring 1999), 136-150.

from the atomized thinking of modernist thought, which seeks to understand from the ground up, piece by separate piece, and instead, try to understand the totality of creation, not as separate pieces in a linear construct, but as a universal, interconnected whole that requires total, simultaneous, and multidirectional understanding, where discrete parts are an illusion, where all parts are not parts at all, but various differing expressions of the same whole. The ideas he put forward in various papers and presentations, while numerous, were not conceived in a vacuum. Taylor had his own personal worldview that he developed over time. His writings often read as elaborate brainstorming sessions or thought experiments, ending with more questions than answers. While it would be impossible to discuss in a single thesis all of Taylor's individual ideas, I firmly believe that even with adequate length, it would be doing them a disservice to discuss them piecemeal or as a Catechistic list, as his ideas and the worldview that backed them were concerned first and foremost with the notion of holism.

The notion that there is a primordial connection between everything is at the heart of Taylor's thought. Networks and interconnectedness are front and centre and archives form the backbone of these networks. From human life to swirling galaxies, for Taylor, all was not only connected, but connected archivally. Archives were thus not a mere collection of evidence or heritage, but an integral part of the universe's very nature, wherein to archive is a religious and cathartic experience. This philosophy was and continues to be important for archival theory in several ways. Taylor rarely gave specifics on how to implement his philosophy, or what someone adopting it would actually *do* in concrete terms. I believe this to be intentional. I believe he viewed the notion that a thought had a beginning and an end, and that it could be rendered as simply as "do X and Y will happen," to be the by-product of the industrialized, atomized era of print media that he so adamantly believed had to be overcome. As such, his ideas are rarely "finished", but they provide something that I believe to be more important than that: they provide a new way of thinking; a way for archivists, communities, and the general public to conceive of their world, themselves, archives, and the relationship between all three in a radically different way, a way that teaches holistic thinking, community-based thinking and ecological thinking. Taylor's contribution to archival theory is thus a series of redefinitions: the redefinition of knowledge, the redefinition of reality, and the redefinition of archives.

These are not truly separate redefinitions, as all of Taylor's thoughts are connected, but rather three tips of an immense and cosmic iceberg drifting in the oceans of time and space. Indeed, Taylor's ideas, as they appeared in published and presented papers, were but bleed over from the primordial ocean of thought that swirled around in his mind. No matter the "thesis" of these mental bleed-overs – as if a single point could be adequately stated without being born of and generating an infinite array of related points and ideas that spin off in every direction – Taylor somehow managed to connect it to his vision of reality. Whether discussing a topic as 'academically appropriate' as Medieval English Law or something as seemingly trivial and unrelated as the Hasbro toys "Transformers" or the divide between Luke Skywalker and Darth Vader, Hugh Taylor was somehow able to adapt and include it as part of his worldview, a worldview that encompassed everything from ecology to spirituality to communicative technology and the media of record. This is because Taylor's worldview was not a list of bullet points, but a network of perceptions creating a flexible and dynamic whole. Everything was connected as a pan-spatial and pan-temporal whole: mind and body, the subatomic and the universal, past, present and future, act and deed, and letter and spirit. At the centre of this holistic worldview were archives, which acted for Taylor as a spine to his philosophical nerve centre. I believe that if Taylor ever did try to articulate this archival network, so paradoxically transcendent while at the same time omnipresent, using a single word of the clumsy and reductive tool we call language, he settled for the word "God". However, before addressing these redefinitions, it is important to take a look at the history of Taylor's papers as they were written.

Taylor's Writings.

While there is not enough space in this short subsection of a chapter to review Taylor's writings one by one, it is important to provide a narrative of their production and the changes that took place between them at various milestones in his writing career. This positions them within Taylor's life and evolving worldview. This section will highlight a selection of Taylor's works that best illustrate the temporal progression of his thoughts.

As has been shown in the previous two chapters, while Taylor's archival writing did not start in earnest until he moved to Canada in 1965, he wrote several papers prior to his archival career that require attention. The first such paper to be considered, though far from an academic piece, nonetheless reflects Taylor's developing worldview. It is a short descriptive piece written in 1943 during his RAF deployment in Tunisia and entitled "Beauty in Everyday North African Life".[3] It shows early on how Taylor's views differed from the norm of European society, even while being influenced by and having been born from that society. Long before being introduced to Marshall McLuhan or any postmodern corpus of ideas, Taylor was considering the subjectivity of culturally

---

[3] NSA, Taylor Archive, MG 1, Vol. 2968, FD 2, "Beauty in Everyday North African Life", 1943.

constructed language, asking that his readers (his parents and close friends) "consider the meaning of the word 'beauty'". And while portions of this piece read as fairly typical European travel writing, complete with all the cultural and colonial baggage such writings usually include, there are some fairly progressive, forward-thinking ideas in it, such as the view that lack of beauty in North Africa from a European perspective "reflects a lack of understanding on our [European] part", rather than "a lack of culture on theirs". Consciousness of subjectivity within thoughts and terms such as "beauty", even though not framed in Foucauldian, discursive terms, shows that Taylor was, on some levels, consistent with what would become postmodernism, poststructuralism, and postcolonial theory.[4]

    Taylor began writing academically while attending Oxford, both for his courses and extracurricular purposes. As mentioned in the previous chapter, he had debated with an archeologist the value of myth and its historical relevance, arguing against its use.[5] This is surprising, given Taylor's later insistence on the value of myth (as will be discussed below), and given the previously mentioned piece written in Tunisia that showed an openness to what would later become postmodern concepts. This shows a number of things about Taylor while at Oxford. First, it shows that while Oxford opened his mind in many other ways, in some ways it actually closed it. Taylor was a product of his academic environment and the positivist, modernist tilt in academia at the time had to have influenced him. Second, it shows how that Taylor's philosophy continued to evolve well into his adult life. It is for this reason that he was able to look back at this speech in

---

[4] Ibid.
[5] NSA, Taylor Archive, MG 1, Vol. 2955, FD 1, Hugh Taylor's speech at the Tenmantle Dinner, 1949.

his memoirs and comment that in those days he lacked a true understanding of myth.[6]

As well at Oxford, Taylor's writings show his developing love affair with local history as well as a love for documentary and bibliographic heritage. In 1947 he wrote a paper about Richard de Bury, the 14th century author of *The Philobiblon*, generally considered to be one of the first books written about librarianship in depth.[7] The following year Taylor authored a paper titled "Tynemouth Priory: A Cell of St. Albans?"[8] which not only illustrates his interest in local history, but also his interest in the history of the church. As discussed in the previous chapter, this interest led him to discover his passion for archives as he wrote his history of Christ Church North Shields and prepared the exhibition for its 300th anniversary. In a retrospective piece written for the Australian Society of Archivists' journal *Archives and Manuscripts* in 1993, Taylor described how his appreciation for specialization had grown throughout his early career:

> I have a deep admiration for those who devote their whole career to one community; their immense local knowledge is not readily available in any other way save through themselves. No software technology will ever match them. My own fate was to be a moving generalist, but there will, I hope, always be room for both kinds in the profession, with other mixes in between.[9]

This love of the local stayed with Taylor throughout his career. It is one of the reasons he left the national stage for Nova Scotia. It was integral to his philosophy.

Taylor wrote less while working at the various local archives in Britain, save for the numerous speeches and presentations he gave and his abandoned attempt to move forward academically by applying to a Ph.D. program. But we should note again here one such presentation given while City Archivist of Liverpool. He used lantern slides and

---

[6] JSJT, file 5, 40:00.
[7] NSA, Taylor Archive, MG 1, Vol. 2968, FD 3, "Richard de Bury", 1947.
[8] Ibid., "Tynemouth Priory: A Cell of St. Albans?".
[9] Taylor, "A Life in Archives: Retrospect and Prospect", 215.

timed music to create a visual history of the city that was designed to make the audience both understand the history intellectually and feel it emotionally. This shows Taylor's developing interest in emotionally charged history, which had existed since his early childhood, and his developing interest in non-textual media of record.

His next major writings, and the first one that can be indisputably labelled as influential, was a short reflective piece written in 1967 just after becoming editor of *The Canadian Archivist*. It was presented to the annual gathering of the Archives Section at the Canadian Historical Association (CHA) and entitled "Archives in Britain and Canada – Impressions of an Immigrant".[10] This paper was important both personally for Taylor and for the Canadian archival profession as a whole, as it grappled with the different views in Canada and Britain on the professional identity of archivists and their roles in society. The British model, following Hilary Jenkinson, saw archivists as objective professionals devoid of any interest in the records beyond professional, curatorial considerations.[11] Canadian archivists saw themselves primarily as historians. Taylor attempted here to reconcile these differing approaches, as he began to merge them into a new hybridized concept. While Canadian archivists were interested in the "raw material of history"[12], Taylor was interested in importing from Britain the idea that archivists were their own profession, different from historians. This reflected and influenced an emerging Canadian view, as it is no coincidence that the Association of Canadian Archivists was established behind Taylor's key leadership a few years after this article was published. At the same time, however, Taylor was not dismissing the Canadian approach outright. He found it had many positive aspects, particularly the willingness of

---

[10] Taylor, "Archives in Britain and Canada – Impressions of an Immigrant", 22-33.
[11] See for example Hilary Jenkinson, *A Manual of Archive Administration* (Oxford: Clarendon Press, 1922).
[12] Taylor, "Archives in Britain and Canada – Impressions of an Immigrant", 24.

Canadian archivists to go beyond the written record to embrace other forms of media, such as photographs. Taylor reflected on this paper in 2000, critiquing himself essentially for being too focused on the semantics of terminology between the British and Canadian traditions, but as he also correctly noted, this focus on language allows one to open up to deconstruction that language and thus gain better insight into why that language is the way it is and what that means for archivists.[13] In short, context becomes important, and it became important for Taylor, as for others, thereafter.

This emerging interest in context was reiterated in 1969 in another speech given to the Archives Section of the CHA. Taylor expanded on his previous call for British archival principles to be taken into consideration by the Canadian archival profession by advocating for the creation of administrative histories that detailed the provenance or administrative structure and context of an organization's archival records.[14] Administrative histories or contextual information about the origins of the records were taken more seriously in Britain at the time than in Canada, with its focus on historical content information in the records with the historian in mind. Taylor pointed out that

> The trouble [in ignoring administrative histories] is that few of the records series are adequately articulated; the relationship between them may be largely unknown and their significance within the context of the whole record group may be lost. We need to know their administrative history, to be reminded that they were created by people to serve a particular purpose in the administration, and we should know the chain of command in any department and evaluate the records accordingly. In short, we cannot accurately arrange or assess the significance of a department's records until we understand thoroughly how it works.[15]

By today's archival standards, this seems obvious and is reflected within the various national and international archival description standards such as Canada's *Rules for*

---

[13] Ibid., 42.
[14] Hugh A. Taylor, "Administrative History: An Archivists' Need", *The Canadian Archivist* Vol. 2 No. 1 (1970), 4-9.
[15] Ibid., 5.

Archival Description (RAD) and the International Council of Archives' (ICA) *General International Standard Archival Description* (ISAD(g)).

While the previous two papers were certainly influential and forward thinking, it was not until 1978 that Taylor's writing began to deviate drastically from the archival norm. Taylor's previous works had elements that differentiated them from those of his peers, such as his focus on big picture ideas rather than the specifics of implementation, and a writing style that was more suited to a collegial, philosophical discussion or brainstorming session than an academic lecture. But they were nonetheless more or less rooted in the mainstream of archival practice, albeit a hybrid of British and Canadian archival practices. This can be seen clearly in his interview for the position of Provincial Archivist of Alberta in 1965. When asked what sorts of records he was most interest in, Taylor responded:

> I am primarily interested in historical records and most of my professional time is spent dealing with local archives from the twelfth century onwards. A very large part of these records consists of collections from country estates and early business enterprises. There are, in addition, the records of country government dating from 1595. At the same time I am concerned that an archivist should at some point interest himself at least in the problems of managing semi-current records, and by his advice, ensure that the classes of records finally deemed historical shall be adequate and coherent, faithfully reflecting the institution which produced them. The tragedy of so much historical record is its scrappiness, hence my interest in the management side.[16]

This response shows how Taylor was still very much mired in the practices of Jenkinsonian archiving, with textual records being *the* records that one should be concerned with.

After discovering Marshall McLuhan, however, and after his revelatory experience with the Siksika (Blackfoot) medicine bundle back in Alberta, Taylor's

---

[16] NSA, Taylor Archive, MG 1, Vol. 2985, FD 4, Hugh A. Taylor, to R.O. Harrison, 1965.

writings and the types of records that he discussed changed dramatically. This did not happen overnight, or even within the year. In fact, Taylor published a paper about McLuhan and what archivists could learn from him about a decade after these experiences. And what they could learn is that understanding the media of record is just as important as understanding the content of the record.[17] This delay may have been due in large part to the fact that the archival world at first did not know what to make of Taylor's new found obsession with McLuhan – his "McLuhanisms", as he phrased it.[18] That was a problem that Taylor had to deal with as he became increasingly interested in the abstract and the cosmic. He first gave a talk about McLuhan and archives in 1976 at the annual conference of the Society of American Archivists (SAA), but the audience was rather unresponsive, and no one was interested in its publication. The American journal *Georgia Archivist* eventually agreed to publish it, given that he was the vice president of the SAA at the time. As Taylor put it, "space was found for a subject which at the time stirred very few hearts in our profession".[19]

Taylor continued down this path of cosmic adventuring into the 1980s and early 1990s, gaining philosophical strength from McLuhan's focus on the immediacy of the emerging electronic and subsequent information age that reintroduced aspects of orality that had been lost during the industrialized, typographic society.[20] New media were discussed in an attempt to provide archivists with specific media literacy, while also attempting to dethrone textual records from their typeset throne. "Documentary Art and the Role of the Archivist" in 1979 sought to 'rescue' art from being thought of as non-

---

[17] Taylor, "The Media of Record: Archives in the Wake of McLuhan".
[18] Ibid., 73.
[19] Ibid.
[20] Marshall McLuhan, "The Medium is the Message" in Kelly Askew and Richar R. Wilk, eds., *The Anthropology of Media* (Malden MA: Blackwell Publishing, 2002), 23.

archival, while 1992's opening address at the "Documents that Move and Speak Symposium" sought to do the same for motion pictures.[21] This coincided perfectly with the emergence of an archival crisis concerning digital records, their archival needs and value. Taylor tackled these topics, as he always did, from a high vantage point, theorizing and imagining possibilities while frequently citing McLuhan and other non-archival theorists for inspiration. He drew it from cultural historian Thomas Berry in 1990's "The Totemic Universe: Appraising the Documentary Future", and from psychologist Ralph Metzner in 1993's "Recycling the Past: The Archivist in the Age of Ecology".[22] Taylor's eclecticism and openness to different ways of thinking allowed him to be at the forefront of the academic shift away from the previously ubiquitous and hegemonic positivist modernity to a more postmodern philosophy. As Taylor himself put it, "I found myself catapulted into the world of postmodernity before that term became common, and long before I knew what it meant!" [23]

But not everyone in the archival profession was on board with this shift, at least not at first. As mentioned above, Taylor's initial "McLuhanisms" got little traction at first. One of the difficult things about being early to the proverbial postmodern party is that many of his archival contemporaries either had little to no grasp of what he was talking about or were actively opposed to it. After one of Taylor's papers during a 1988 Association of Canadian Archivists' conference session entitled "Towards the New Archivist: The Integrated Professional?" – a paper that sought to describe the roles

---

[21] Hugh A. Taylor, "Documentary Art and the Role of the Archivist", *The American Archivist* 42 (October 1979):417-428; and Hugh A. Taylor, "Opening Address to the 'Documents that Move and Speak' Symposium", in Cook and Dodds, eds., *Imagining Archives: Essays and Reflections by Hugh A. Taylor*, 184-197.
[22] Hugh A. Taylor, "The Totemic Universe: Appraising the Documentary Future" in Cook and Dodds, eds., *Imagining Archives: Essays and Reflections by Hugh A. Taylor*, 15-29; Hugh A. Taylor, "Recycling the Past: The Archivist in the Age of Ecology", *Archivaria* 35 (Spring 1993): 203-213.
[23] Taylor, "The Media of Record: Archives in the Wake of McLuhan", 72.

archivists might adopt going into the 1990s -- Luciana Duranti delivered a scathing rejection of the postmodern concepts that Taylor had been writing about since the 1970s, as the following rather dramatic excerpt shows:

> Contradictions, one after another...this is our beloved Hugh with his most mischievous mask. You love contradictions, don't you? They make people go crazy, and in their disorientation, in their desperate search for a way out, they may gain some new insight...Hugh loves to play. He has been in the thick of the fight for so many years that now he just wants to sit on a cloud like Jove, throwing thunderbolts among the poor mortals and watching them running around in opposite directions...And, of course, in tune with the rest of the paper, Hugh does not clearly state his case because he is lured away again by his love of paradox...Hugh, resuming the ancient methodology of mathematician-philosopher, uses [paradoxes] as a strategy to confuse the minds which, stirred by the need of overcoming the confusion, may become creative and identify new solutions. Even so, I do not think that it is fair to ask questions without offering answers and to speak by paradoxes without making proposals for their resolutions.[24]

While this is perhaps an extreme example of the critique Taylor faced, it shows the kind of criticism that Taylor drew. Taylor accepted the criticism and internalized it, not as doubt about his ideas or thought processes, but in creating his self-identification as a thinker. In 1980 Taylor had, with some external coaxing, written an archival manual, something, with its positivist listings of near objective rules and guidelines, was rather distant from Taylor's typical style or enthusiasm, and it was evident in the final product, as mentioned by its reviewers[25], and by Taylor himself, who rather playfully referred to himself as an authority on textbooks, having published "a particularly bad one".[26] In his final reminiscence, written just a few years before he died, Taylor delivered a rather detailed self-critique of his own philosophy and writing style, but in which he apologized for none of it (another of Taylor's beloved paradoxes):

---

[24] Transcript from the Association of Canadian Archivists' Annual Conference, Session: "Towards the New Archivist: The Integrated Professional?", June 8, 1988, Windsor, Ontario, pages 1-4.
[25] See J. Robert Davison, *Archivaria* 14 (Summer 1982): 181-183.
[26] Taylor, "Afterword: On Reflection and Imagination", 248.

> I do not have that mix of Plato and Aristotle...characteristic of Terry Cook, Luciana Duranti, Terry Eastwood, Tom Nesmith, Brien Brothman, and Richard Brown, to name but a few Canadians, with their generous wealth of footnotes supporting theoretical structures and action research. To be honest, I suppose I do more thinking than reading in a search for connections which link the work of others to archives and thereby reveal unexplored relationships through "probes" in the McLuhan tradition – which may touch on a useful revelation or spin wildly off track. My citations appear to range widely, far beyond the boundaries of archivy, but they are not carefully selected from groups of Dewey decimals or Library of Congress alpha-numerical schémas. Rather they are the product of the "new book" shelves which I devour for their stimulating freshness.[27]

And while this provocativeness and refusal to deliver 'concrete' terms and solutions drew criticism, these ideas and approaches made Taylor revolutionary in archival theory. Terry Cook, for example, upon Taylor's death, opened his obituary by stating that the archival world had lost one of its "giants".[28] As well, many other archivists have used Taylor's ideas, built upon them, and created new and imaginative ideas of their own. Elizabeth Yakel, for example, relied heavily on Taylor to posit that archival reference services should be seen not as spaces of knowledge delivery, but as spaces of knowledge creation.[29] Laura Miller also drew on Taylor when characterizing the development of the total archives concept, tying in Taylor's insistence on holism and totality, referencing him so many times that the history of total archives almost looks synonymous with the history of Taylor.[30]

Taylor had no qualms about expanding archival theory to embrace his other interests. As the title itself suggests, the previously mentioned "Recycling the Past" features Taylor's environmental interests and his seminal "The Archivist, the Letter, and

---

[27] Ibid., 248-249.
[28] Cook, "Hugh A. Taylor, 1920-2005", 275.
[29] See Elizabeth Yakel, "Thinking Inside and Outside the Boxes: Archival Reference Services at the Turn of the Century", *Archivaria* 49 (Spring 2000): 140-160.
[30] See Laura Miller, "Discharging our Debt: The Evolution of the Total Archives Concept in English Canada", *Archivaria* 46 (Fall 1998): 103-146.

the Spirit", the final published academic paper of his career, wove religion and metaphysics into the archival fold so expertly that one could characterize it as a theological or ontological paper rather than simply as an archival paper. Indeed, these articles were no smokescreen or Trojan horse that sought to sneak non-archival theorizing into archival journals and conferences at the expense of archives. Rather, as will be seen below, in Taylor's eyes, nothing was off topic when it came to archives. He firmly believed in the complete integration of ideas into a cohesive whole, where disciplinary divisions were artificial chasms, waiting to be bridged or, as he rather eloquently put it: "I've always tried to build bridges of communication as my father built bridges for railways [and I've always seen] records as the products or artifacts of people trying to communicate."[31] It is with this in mind – communication as bedrock – that we now turn to Taylor's significance in archival theory: the uplifting of archival theory and practice to cosmic, quasi-religious significance through the redefinition of knowledge, reality, and, finally, archives.

Redefining Knowledge

To begin with the redefinition of knowledge, it would be a gross oversimplification to say that this part of his worldview developed before the others or that the others were the result of this redefinition, but it nonetheless serves as a way into the rest of Taylor's worldview. This redefinition revolves around Taylor's discovery of Marshall McLuhan and the revelation that Taylor saw in him. Most important to archival theory is the legitimization – or perhaps liberation – of knowledge and epistemes that differ from the hegemonic industrial-modernist model that had dominated academic discourse, archival or otherwise, since the 19th century. Taylor not only argued against

---
[31] JSJT, file 6, 8:30.

the aforementioned model's right to hegemony, but called for the need to embrace a new episteme, one he would refer to as both "new-tribalism" and "new-orality", terms derived from McLuhan's at the time (and to some degree, still) controversial thoughts on the role communication plays in human development, perception and thought.

Just as Marx theorized human development in terms of modes of production, McLuhan, in *The Gutenberg Galaxy*, theorized them in terms of modes of communication, with particular modes yielding particular socio-cultural results.[32] Since the written word caused humanity to internalize communication, individualism came to prominence, and when the printing press codified and manufactured that writing by use of automated conformity, industrialization and modernism arose. Given that electronic forms of communication were on the rise, a new society would emerge, one which would revitalize the connectivity of oral communication and knowledge that had been lost (by certain cultures): "the new electronic interdependence recreates the world in the image of a global village."[33] In another seminal work, *Understanding Media*, McLuhan focused his attention on characteristics of the media itself and coined the now famous phrase, "The medium is the message", referring to how more than the content contained within any given medium, the form it takes informs and elaborates on the sociocultural context in which it was created.[34]

Never one to miss how new ideas related to the world of archives, Taylor latched onto McLuhan quite tightly, realizing then what now seems obvious: that the media of record are in themselves necessarily the archivist's concern. But Taylor's most important

---

[32] Marshall McLuhan, *The Gutenberg Galaxy; The Making of Typographic Man* (Toronto: University of Toronto Press, 1962).
[33] Ibid., 31.
[34] Marshall McLuhan, *Understanding Media: The Extensions of Man* (Corte Madera CA: Gingko Press, 2003).

takeaway from McLuhan was his prophetical foretelling of how the industrial-modernist model, based on principles of industrialism, individualism, atomization and literality – all attributes inherited from the print media mode of communication that lay at its foundation – was, along with the printed word, nearing the end of its hegemony. Electronic communications such as radio, television and punch-card computing, according to McLuhan, were set to replace their predecessors and thus readjust the balance of human sensory perception. This new mode of communication, McLuhan wrote, would be one which "mingles the cultures of prehistory with the dregs of industrial marketeers, the nonliterate with the semiliterate and the postliterate".[35] Or, as Taylor expressed it in his 1988 article "'My Very Act and Deed': Some Reflections on the Role of Textual Records in the Conduct of Affairs": "we are beginning to move into a 'post-literate' mode which, while not dispensing with literacy, reintroduces the immediacy of rapid interactive networking and feedback analogous to oral exchange."[36] This new mode of communication would bring about a sort of renaissance for orality in which our sensory balance would adjust accordingly.

The ultimate gain of this new-orality, for Taylor, was the rediscovery of a holistic method of thought that only the immediacy of orality (or new-orality) could offer. The differences between this new-orality and print-based thought are many. Taylor once famously compared new-orality-based thinking and print-based thinking to the Hasbro Transformer toys and to jigsaw puzzles stating:

> The most ingenious [Transformers] are designed all of a piece as ambiguous constructs filled with options ranging from robots to rockets to racing cars; the pattern changes, the meaning changes, the information changes, but the data - the

---

[35] Marshall McLuhan, "The Medium is the Message" in Askew and Wilk, *The Anthropology of Media*, 23.
[36] Hugh A. Taylor, "'My Very Act and Deed': Some Reflections on the Role of Textual Records in the Conduct of Affairs.", *American Archivist* 51 (Fall 1988): 457.

> given "bits" - remain the same. Contrast this with the jigsaw puzzle fractured into a thousand separate pieces which has only one solution, one answer, one option. The jigsaw is also popular, but its form is very much a product of the industrial age, mass produced, interlocking with very similarly shaped pieces but fitting correctly only in one place.[37]

The difference, then, is one of the right brain versus the left, holistic thinking versus atomized thinking. This holistic thinking, Taylor puts forward, echoing McLuhan, is a characteristic of oral societies (or at least, those with an oral sensory alignment) and will re-emerge in the age of new-orality as communication becomes more immediate, participatory and concrete, moving away from the highly abstract and transcendent communication associated with print. This shift from atomized thinking to holistic thinking will (and in some areas) has already begun to redefine how we perceive the past. The most important example of this is Taylor's plea for myth as a legitimate – and in many ways superior – form of knowledge.

Taylor's defence of myth, as expressed in 1978 in his "The Media of Record" is in stark contrast to the debate that he had engaged in while at Oxford when he decried myth as being unreliable. Now, as an older and wiser man chocked full of "McLuhanisms", Taylor's position on myth had reversed and, using McLuhan as the base of his reasoning, Taylor vigorously defended myth as an epistemological methodology. In the article, Taylor defines myth as "the holistic perception of a complex evolution that ordinarily extended over time."[38] This is contrary to the more traditional "scientific" method of understanding the past, which is abstracted, analytical and divorced from its subject: an empirical examination of a point or segment on the quantifiable straight line from past to

---

[37] Hugh. A. Taylor, "Transformation in the Archives: Technological Adjustment or Paradigm Shift?", *Archivaria* 25 (Winter 1987-1988): 12.
[38] Taylor, "The Media of Record: Archives in the Wake of McLuhan", 66.

present, a line that infinitely approaches the present without ever truly touching it.[39] This conceptual separation of past from present is, by Taylor, relegated to the purview of historians who, as those who by definition freeze the past, thereby tearing it from the present, appear as anachronisms in Taylor's writings.[40] While it is unlikely that Taylor believed historians as a whole were guilty of this, at the time he wrote the article, postmodern ideas and challenges to "scientific", "objective" history were still a decade away from entering the mainstream among historians.

The chief example used by Taylor to show the anachronism of "freezing" is the Bible. The Bible, if taken entirely literality, is damaging both to itself, as critics take delight in pointing out its various inconsistencies, and to others, as many fundamentalists use it to support intolerant worldviews. The Bible, however, a document whose content seems to some to be 'frozen', is actually the result of successive attempted 'freezings', rather than of a single moment of creation. It is based on various writings much older than itself and a plethora of oral traditions, compiled and edited by countless individuals over a great span of time. In the act of freezing these long practised oral traditions in writing, they lose what Taylor refers to as "permanent value" – the lessons and insights at their core, or their ultimate meaning.[41] They become literalized, reduced to a binary object that is either true or false.[42] The 'frozen' Bible is viewed as such through the eyes of the industrial-modernist who seeks to preserve its literality rather than its permanent value.

---

[39] Taylor gives an expanded analysis of "scientific" history in Taylor, "My Very Act and Deed: Some Reflections on the Role of Textual Records in the Conduct of Affairs.", 458.
[40] Hugh A. Taylor, "The Media of Record: Archives in the Wake of McLuhan", 69.
[41] Taylor, "The Totemic Universe: Appraising the Documentary Future", 163.
[42] Taylor, "The Archivist, the Letter, and the Spirit", 6-7; and Taylor, "Transformation in the Archives: Technological Adjustment or Paradigm Shift", 17.

Redefining Reality

While Taylor's McLuhan-inspired redefinition of knowledge was certainly controversial at the time, it has gained far more acceptance by today's scholars, both within archival theory and outside it, as postmodernism has spread throughout. Far more radical is Taylor's redefinition of reality, which he expressed often in ecological or religious terms, sometimes both. As already discussed, Taylor had a knack for being able to look at seemingly unrelated or tangentially related subjects and to find ways in which they were relevant to archival theory. The reverse was also true: he managed to see how archival theory connected to everything: the senses, thought, life, even existence itself. He sought to bore right down to the fabric of creation and to see how the fibers that bound it together were archival in the sense that they showed a complex web of contextual relationships, connecting everything from the entirety of the cosmos to the smallest of subatomic particles:

> If we take the universe and its Creator, or the scientific concept of the "Big Bang" theory as the beginning of cosmic evolution, then cosmogenesis, the creation moment, becomes the ultimate context of all matter as it moves down through the galaxies, nebulae, planets, and stars to life in all its forms on our own planet; all creation is connected in various ways in a marvelous spatial balance.[43]

Everything that exists, then, is a form of communication, including humanity, whose nature is largely determined by our genetic encoding, a code that, like Taylor's RAF training taught him, was waiting to be broken. Practising what he had preached,[44] Taylor paid attention to the media of record; he had not ignored it or taken it for granted as a meaningless carrier of content. If the medium is the message, then the message, as

---

[43] Ibid., 5-6.
[44] Taylor, "The Media of Record: Archives in the Wake of McLuhan", 66.

seen by Taylor, is humanity.[45] As binary code comes together and aligns itself in various electronic dances to create the electronic forms of communication most of us use daily, DNA and genetic code performs a similar dance of alignment, creating various unique forms of life[46]. Life is thus, for Taylor, an archive of communicative memory, an expression of Creation itself, what some, Taylor included, refer to as God. This God is not a transcendent one, divorced from creation,[47] but is the reflexive existence of existence -- the Creation that created creation, be it by intelligence or happenstance, and its very personification. All of creation is thus a part of this God – items linked archivally to one another in a fluid network we call the universe. This train of thought harkens back to Taylor's strong ties to ecumenical Christianity, where all Christian churches are related in Christ and therefore are as one. So, too, is all creation related archivally by provenance and thus, all creation is ultimately a single interrelated web of being, and religiously sacrosanct in its own right.

This way of thinking directly relates to Taylor's fascination with the holistic immediacy of orality. Where written and printed word abstracted communication and thus created a worldview based on transcendence, orality dealt more concretely and holistically. Orality itself, of course, is a form of abstraction: language is as transcendent a way of expressing thought as the written word is of expressing language, but short of ESP or the development of a hive mind, it is the most holistic form of expression that can be mustered and certainly the electronic technology behind new-orality can provide certain modes of holistic expression that not even orality proper could. In any case,

---

[45] Taylor, "The Archivist, the Letter, and the Spirit", 6.
[46] Taylor, "The Totemic Universe: Appraising the Documentary Future", 164.
[47] Taylor provides a list compiled by Thomas Berry that lists and critiques the 5 transcendences in the Western-print worldview, the first of which is a transcendent deity. It thus seems unlikely to me that Taylor would himself believe in transcendent deity, but rather one connected to Creation. See Ibid., 165.

Taylor's notion of the God of archival creation coincided with another passion of his: the need for environmental preservation.

If Creation is an archive of the most cosmic scale, then its destruction or the destruction of any of its various parts is a matter of archival preservation. Taylor lamented about the resultant archival loss that came about from the desacralized state in which the industrial-modernist worldview had placed the environment, stating in his 1990 "The Totemic Universe":

> we are losing 20,000 species of plant and animal life a year irreversibly, which is like tearing that number of pages from the book of life. We have irretrievably lost this information which could be self-perpetuating and evolving. Is this not more valuable than some forms of information which librarians and archivists struggle to preserve?[48]

This plea coincides with the goals expressed by the Veterans for Nuclear Disarmament Committee, as mentioned in the previous chapter, in its call for conflicting sides (in this case, all the sides humanity has to offer) to unite and put aside their differences for the greater archival good: preservation of the records of Creation.

This plea also coincides with Taylor's views on myth and literality by favouring replication and the preservation of what is permanently valuable over an attempt to freeze in time and literalize. It was imperative, then, (and still is) that humanity "recognize the organic context of our lives and recover a sense of community that is in harmony with the 'story of the universe'", lest "immensely powerful interests now driving an obsolete and discredited modernism…render the planet uninhabitable"[49].

Redefining Archives

This leads to Taylor's final redefinition, that of archives themselves. This

---

[48] Ibid.
[49] Taylor, "The Archivist, the Letter, and the Spirit", 12.

redefinition is the culmination of the first two and sees the archivist's role in Taylor's redefined knowledge and reality to be that of the shaman: a figure beholden to a community or communities and one who helps build communities as a keeper (in Taylor's words) of tribal knowledge.[50] By this Taylor, echoing McLuhan, refers to the "group-oriented characteristics" of oral and new-oral cultures in opposition to the "intense individualism of typographic" humanity.[51] Indeed, Taylor sees archives as the descendants of these shamanic keepers of oral knowledge, noting that, like oral knowledge, archives are by nature "organic, not classified, forms of information, closely related to actions and decisions".[52] Archiving, then, is by its very nature a community activity with religious implications, and archivists are the religious keepers of community values and memory. Their role is not to impose classification, but to discern patterns, not to preserve by literally 'freezing' the records in time, but by preserving that which the community deems permanently valuable. Archives ought not to seem to transcend humanity as remote static storehouses of the records of a fast receding past, but embrace and serve the community's key contemporary needs (such as protection of the environment) as an integral part of the community.

Taylor's future vision of archivists embracing their shamanistic roles in the new-oral culture is, by his own admission, idealistic,[53] but it has value as it provides archivists and communities with a different way of thinking about themselves: the knowledge that archiving does not have to be the job of an invisible individual, divorced from the community while imposing his or her own classifications on the community's knowledge,

---

[50] Taylor, "The Media of Record: Archives in the Wake of McLuhan", 68.
[51] Ibid., 67.
[52] Taylor, "The Totemic Universe: Appraising the Documentary Future", 166-167.
[53] Taylor, "Recycling the Past: The Archivist in the Age of Ecology", 210.

following the latest manual of atomized rules one-by-one, living the role of Koheleth of the biblical Book of Ecclesiastes, crying "vanity of vanities!" as the minutes on the clock slowly tick by. Rather, Taylor envisions a world where communities and the environment are one harmonious organ, bioregions speckling the globe. The information therein "including oral history, folklore, and the archives of families, business, and institutions will," according to Taylor, "find a natural home in the community archives where all can feel and experience a dynamic heritage experience in which they can be personally involved, and which will be passed down to their descendants".[54] In this future, Taylor sees archivists shedding the confines of professional isolation and the atomized specialization of labour associated with typographic society, accepting that their work requires "total involvement" and "a healthy mix of experiences which embraces all our senses".[55]

This depiction of archiving goes beyond a mere profession and approaches something almost sacred, satisfying the dual role of the shaman as both keeper of knowledge and a religious figure. Indeed, Taylor often used religious language to describe archiving and archivists. He refers to archivists as being prophetic, refers to himself as an unrepentant convert of McLuhan's philosophy, describes the relationship of living creatures to one another as "divine" and makes countless references to the Bible.[56] But these were more than just words for Taylor. In "The Archivist, the Letter, and the Spirit", arguably Taylor's most personal piece of writing, he moves religion from subtext to subject as he connects perhaps the most important thread of the tapestry that is his worldview. In this article, Taylor refers to Richard Klumpenhouwer's description of

---

[54] Taylor, "The Archivist, the Letter, and the Spirit", 13.
[55] Taylor, "The Media of Record: Archives in the Wake of McLuhan", 68.
[56] Ibid., 69, 73; and Taylor, "The Totemic Universe: Appraising the Documentary Future", 164, 163.

work in archives as a religious experience, one which involved a "quasi-religious initiation into an archival culture" and required him to take a sort of metaphorical pilgrimage to "climb the mountain of archival exploration" which he found to be "a powerful expression of humanity".[57] Klumpenhouwer then goes on to describe how he felt he became part "of a larger mission, a community, a professional culture that believes in archives", concluding "In the end, it is a faith based on identity with something bigger than yourself. And if that is not a religion, I do not know what is."[58]

The two key words in that expression are "religion" and "community". Archives are not simply useful to communities, but are one in and of themselves. In addition, by their nature as community knowledge, they beget new communities; communities form around them as they formed around religious temples in ancient Sumer. The networks and relationships within and between these communities then form their own archives which go on to form new communities in an archival Ouroboros of infinite self-reflexivity. It is for this reason that Taylor always had a soft spot in his heart for local archivists and local historians, those who knew their community inside out and could fulfil the role of shamanic keeper of community knowledge. In Taylor's view, archivists have for too long rejected this role of religious significance. In embracing it, archivists can, according to Taylor, find a way by which to ground themselves in their work and think about it holistically, rather than trudging through the monotony of atomized and formulaic repetition.[59] This does not require the belief in Taylor's God, or in any God in the traditional sense of the word, nor does it require one to lead a religious life. It asks that archivists recognize their role within communities, one very much in concert with the

---
[57] Taylor, "The Archivist, the Letter, and the Spirit", 9.
[58] Ibid.
[59] Ibid., 8.

spirit of the community, which has religious significance all its own. According to Taylor, religion can "bind us back" to this role, to archivists' origins as stalwarts of the community's ineffable essence, working in concert with the community and the environment that itself is a spiritual part of the community.[60] In so doing, archives, as the networks that connect communities, their pasts and presents, reify them, and are themselves spiritual essences – one may even refer to them as an aspect of God.

This heady religiosity should come as no surprise, given Taylor's relationship with religion and spirituality. But while religion would, for some, act as a point of division and exclusion, for Taylor it acted as a point of connection. This is the result of Taylor's infinite and unending need to connect with something greater than himself. It can be seen in his connection to the historicity of the architecture in Bath, his connection to military symbolism and through it, to his father, his emotional connection to history as a subject, his role in the ecumenical movement, as well as in his other activist causes, and in his connection to archives. Taylor took all those needs for connection, the cry of one who felt alone as a child, and interpret them through a spiritualist, archival lens that saw the patterns, as an archivist should. This system of beliefs created yet another paradox for Taylor. On the one hand, just as Taylor felt that he was on the "fringes of Anglicanism", his high level, cosmic archival philosophy put him on the fringes of archival theory as well, and a statement made about his role in the ecumenical movement could very much also be adapted and applied to Taylor's life as an archivist: "I did [work] for the Church, but my interest in things ecumenical at that time [the 1950s], put me on the fringe of parish life as being rather odd. I suppose I've always prowled around the frontiers,

---

[60] Ibid., 9.

building connections – bridges."⁶¹ This was true for his religious life, and it became true as well for his life as an archivist, since for Taylor they were one and the same. Thus, perhaps his greatest contribution to the archival world is in suggesting its higher purpose. In many ways, for archivists and those affected by their work, Taylor was a prophet.

Archivists, then, can take away from Taylor (and many already have) a new way of thinking, one which promotes connections, fluidity and harmony over transcendence, rigidity and opposition. It is left to archivists themselves and the communities they represent to determine how to act on Taylor's philosophy, how to implement it and what such a reality would even look like, but this does not detract from Taylor's importance and in some ways, it would be contrary to the spirit of his message. Taylor's philosophy, like the Bible, should not be frozen in literality; the Gospel of Hugh should be treated as such. The cosmic philosopher thinks cosmically and makes others rethink their long held philosophical assumptions and outlooks by asking of them that they just imagine.

---

⁶¹ JSJT, file 6, 29:00.

Conclusion

Hugh Alexander Taylor passed away on September 11, 2005, at the age of eighty-five. He had been battling dementia towards the end of his life, which was exacerbated by the loss of one of his daughters to a heart valve complication at the age of forty-one. According to Daphne Taylor, Hugh could simply no longer handle it.[1] Prior to the onset of his dementia, Taylor had been enjoying retired life in Victoria, returning to archival work occasionally as a consultant. In addition to this, he traveled a lot with his family, going on many a vacation to some new and exciting place, no doubt filled with the possibilities of new ideas that immersion in a different environment often provides.

This thesis has looked at the collective temporal experiences that made Taylor's life, shaping his points of view, his outlook on life, creation, religion, and, most importantly, archives. From his childhood when he struggled with feelings of isolation and his inability to satisfy British society's gendered taxonomy of what a "man" should be, he retreated inward and found new worlds of cosmic proportions to explore. This life of internalization, where thought and emotion blurred and blended into one another, developed for Taylor a unique and imaginative multiverse of infinity where thoughts and ideas swirled about as the ether that existed between worlds and realities. Here, thoughts and ideas could not only be comprehended intellectually, but connected with on an emotional level. This striving for something to feel connected to drove Taylor as a child to feel the history around him, be it from the architectural grandeur of centuries old cathedrals and monasteries, the stunning historical beauty of Bath, or the symbolically charged pageantry of military rituals and parades. The drama that infused daily life while living with his aunt only served to build on what had already been developing in Taylor: a view of life from the vantage point of some cosmic force greater than humanity could dream. There is no sure understanding of what vantage point this was, but it seems that for Taylor this cosmic vantage point was what he referred to as God.

This feeling of wanting to connect with the world around him and the people around him led him to enlist in the war, which introduced him not only to a communal

---

[1] Daphne Taylor, phone interview by author, October 13, 2014.

world where he was able to feel good about himself, but an entirely new language – that of Morse Code – to ponder and remind him that language is a medium in its own right, not just a container of information, whether in written word or audio recordings. When he discovered what Marshall McLuhan had to say about media, this understanding of language was essential to his adaptation of McLuhan's ideas to archives and beyond. But it was Oxford and history that first drew him, or a desire to connect with the past, which he felt constantly swirling around him, begging to be connected with and understood.

If history was the content to connect with, then archives and records, in their various media became the language by which the past spoke. Taylor now had found his calling, to study, understand, and replicate conversations with the past so as to feel it and connect it with the present and the future. He began this in Britain, likely unaware of the full extent of what he would discover about archives in the years to come. It was not until moving to Canada, where he once again would have been out of place and disconnected to a degree, that he began to understand the secret. The holistic approach and sacred regard for the past's words that Taylor witnessed with the Siksika medicine bundles and the life changing discovery of McLuhan finally made it clear to him: that communication is a sacred act of Creation, and as such, archivists are the mystics of the contemporary world, both figuratively in the sense of being access points to sacred knowledge, but also literally, serving the same function as the shaman and the knowledge keeper of society.

Taylor's views were challenging and even bizarre to some, but they inspired a generation of archivists to think beyond the proverbial textbook or how-to manual on archives and to move from simply questioning techniques to questioning the very foundations of archives themselves. Doing so gives archivists a higher purpose. As Terry Cook explains, Taylor's "stimulating ideas and engaging style in his later-career essays provide a bright beacon of hope in time of professional change, technological anxiety, and occasional hubris. That is his legacy; his memorial will be that we seize his torch and carry on his probing and questioning."[2] What archivists can thus learn from Taylor

---

[2] Cook, "Hugh A. Taylor, 1920-2005", 280.

is not any one of his specific ideas, but that archivists should always strive to use their positions for higher purposes than simply receiving paychecks. What archivists do matters, and it deserves to be thought about in a way that honours and encourages that. Taylor brought the cosmos down to Earth, for all to explore.

Bibliography

PRIMARY SOURCES

Association of Canadian Archivists. Transcript from the Association of Canadian Archivists' Annual Conference, Session: "Towards the New Archivist: The Integrated Professional?" June 8, 1988, Windsor, Ontario.

Collins, L.J. "A Call to Christian Action in Public Affairs". *Theology* 50:321 (March, 1947): 91-96.

Provincial Archives of Alberta. "Our History", Provincial Archives of Alberta Website, http://culture.alberta.ca/paa/about/ourhistory.aspx, last accessed April 18, 2016.

Taylor, Daphne. Phone interview by author. October 13, 2014.

Nova Scotia Archives, Taylor Family Archives, MG 1, vols. 2951-2991, 3129-3159, Halifax, Nova Scotia.

Taylor, Hugh A. "Editorial". *The Canadian Archivist.* Vol. 1 No. 3 (1969): 3.

Taylor, Hugh A. "Archives in Britain and Canada – Impressions of an Immigrant". *The Canadian Archivist* Vol. 1, No. 7 (1969): 22-23.

Taylor, Hugh A. "Administrative History: An Archivist's Need". *The Canadian Archivist* Vol. 2, No. 1 (1970): 4-9.

Taylor, Hugh A. "The Provincial Archives of New Brunswick". *Acadiensis* Vol. 1, No. 1 (Autumn 1971): 71-83.

Taylor, Hugh A. "Information Retrieval and the Training of Archivists". *The Canadian Archivist* Vol. 2, No. 3 (1972): 30-35.

Taylor, Hugh A. "Clio in the Raw: Archival Materials and the Teaching of History". *The American Archivist* 35 (July/October 1972): 317-330.

Taylor, Hugh A. "SAA Philadelphia 1975". *Archivaria* 1 (Winter 1975-76): 94-96.

Taylor, Hugh A. "Canadian Archives: Patterns from a Federal Perspective". *Archivaria* 2 (Summer 1976): 3-19.

Taylor, Hugh A. "Oral History and Archives: Keynote Speech to the 1976 Canadian Oral History Conference". *Canadian Oral History Journal* 2 (1976-77): 1-5.

Taylor, Hugh A. "The Discipline of History and the Education of the Archivist". *The American Archivist* 40 (October 1977): 395-402.

Taylor, Hugh A. "The Media of Record: Archives in the Wake of McLuhan" in Cook, Terry and Gordon Dodds, eds. *Imagining Archives: Essays and Reflections by Hugh A. Taylor.* Society of American Archivists and Association of Canadian Archivists in association with Scarecrow Press, 2003.

Taylor, Hugh A. "The Archival Experience in England and Canada." *The Midwestern Archivist* 4, no. 1 (1979): 53-56.

Taylor, Hugh A. "Focus." *The American Archivist* 42 (January 1979): 9-11.

Taylor, Hugh A. "Documentary Art and the Role of the Archivist." *The American Archivist* 42 (October 1979): 551-555.

Taylor, Hugh A. "The Collective Memory: Archives and Libraries as Heritage". *Archivaria* 15 (Winter 1982-1983): 118-130.

Taylor, Hugh A. "'My Very Act and Deed': Some Reflections on the Role of Textual Records in the Conduct of Affairs". *The American Archivist* 51 (Fall 1988): 456-469.

Taylor, Hugh A. "The Totemic Universe: Appraising the Documentary Future" in Cook, Terry and Gordon Dodds, eds. *Imagining Archives: Essays and Reflections by Hugh A. Taylor*. Society of American Archivists and Association of Canadian Archivists in association with Scarecrow Press, 2003.

Taylor, Hugh A. "Chip Monks at the Gate: The Impact of Technology on Archives, Libraries, and the User". *Archivaria* 33 (Winter 1991-1992): 173-180.

Taylor, Hugh A. "Opening Address to the 'Documents That Move and Speak' Symposium" in Cook, Terry and Gordon Dodds, eds. *Imagining Archives: Essays and Reflections by Hugh A. Taylor*. Society of American Archivists and Association of Canadian Archivists in association with Scarecrow Press, 2003.

Taylor, Hugh. "Recycling the Past: The Archivist in the Age of Ecology". *Archivaria* 35 (Spring 1993): 203-213.

Taylor, Hugh A. "A Life in Archives: Retrospect and Prospect". *Archives and Manuscripts* 21 (November 1993): 222-236.

Taylor, Hugh. "The Archivist, the Letter, and the Spirit". *Archivaria* 43 (Spring 1997): 1-16.

Taylor, Hugh A. "Journeys in Space, Journeys in Time: A Poor Attempt at Autobiography". c. 1990s. MPEG 4 Audio. 6 Files.

SECONDARY SOURCES

Askew, Kelly and Richard R. Wilk, eds. *The Anthropology of Media*. Malden MA: Blackwell Publishing, 2002.

Craig, Barbara L., ed. *The Archival Imagination: Essays in Honour of Hugh A. Taylor*. Ottawa: Association of Canadian Archivists, 1992.

Cook, Terry. "The Tyranny of the Medium: A Comment on 'Total Archives'". *Archivaria* 9 (Winter 1979-80): 141-149.

Cook, Terry. "What is Past is Prologue: A History of Archival Ideas Since 1898, and the Future Paradigm Shift". *Archivaria* 43 (Spring 1997): 17-63.

Cook, Terry and Gordon Dodds, eds. *Imagining Archives: Essays and Reflections by Hugh A. Taylor.* Society of American Archivists and Association of Canadian Archivists in association with Scarecrow Press, 2003.

Cook, Terry. "Hugh A. Taylor, 1920-2005". *Archivaria* 60 (Fall 2005): 275-282.

Davison, J. Robert. "Book Review #1: Taylor, 'The Arrangement and Description of Archival Materials'". *Archivaria* 14 (Summer 1982): 181-183.

Eastwood, Terry. "The Origins and Aims of the Master of Archival Studies Programme at the University of British Columbia". *Archivaria* 16 (Summer 1983): 35-52.

Eastwood, Terry. "Attempts at National Planning for Archives in Canada, 1975-1985". *The Public Historian* Vol. 8 No. 3 (Summer 1986): 74-91.

The Education Committee, Association of Canadian Archivists. "Guidelines for the Development of a Two-Year Curriculum for a Master of Archival Studies Programme (December 1988)". *Archivaria* 29 (Winter 1989-1990), 128-141.

Jenkinson, Hilary. *A Manual of Archive Administration.* Oxford: Clarendon Press, 1922.

McLuhan, Marshall. *The Gutenberg Galaxy; the Making of Typographic Man.* Toronto: University of Toronto Press, 1962.

McLuhan, Marshall. *Understanding Media: The Extensions of Man.* New York: McGraw-Hill, 1964.

Miller, Laura. "Discharging Our Debt: The Evolution of the Total Archives Concept in English Canada". *Archivaria* 46 (Fall 1998): 103-146.

Nesmith, Tom. "Still Fuzzy, But More Accurate: Some Thoughts on the 'Ghosts' of Archival Theory". *Archivaria* 47 (Spring 1999), 136-150.

Yakel, Elizabeth. "Thinking Inside and Outside the Boxes: Archival Reference Services at the Turn of the Century". *Archivaria* 49 (Spring 2000): 140-160.

Printed in the USA
CPSIA information can be obtained
at www.ICGtesting.com
LVHW051201230424
778165LV00001B/198